# I WILL TELL NO
# WAR STORIES

Books by Howard Mansfield
*Cosmopolis*
*In the Memory House*
*Skylark*
*The Same Ax, Twice*
*The Bones of the Earth*
*Turn & Jump*
*Dwelling in Possibility*
*Sheds*
*Summer Over Autumn*
*The Habit of Turning the World Upside Down*
*Chasing Eden*

**Editor**
*Where the Mountain Stands Alone*

**For Children**
*Hogwood Steps Out*

# I WILL TELL NO
# WAR STORIES

## WHAT OUR FATHERS LEFT UNSAID
## ABOUT WORLD WAR II

## HOWARD MANSFIELD

LYONS
PRESS

*Essex, Connecticut*

An imprint of Globe Pequot, the trade division of
The Rowman & Littlefield Publishing Group, Inc.
4501 Forbes Blvd., Ste. 200
Lanham, MD 20706
www.rowman.com

Distributed by NATIONAL BOOK NETWORK

British Library Cataloguing in Publication Information available

**Library of Congress Cataloging-in-Publication Data**

Names: Mansfield, Howard, 1957– author.
Title: I will tell no war stories : what our fathers left unsaid about
   World War II / Howard Mansfield.
Other titles: What our fathers left unsaid about World War II
Description: Essex, Connecticut : Lyons Press, [2024] | Includes
   bibliographical references.
Identifiers: LCCN 2023048887 (print) | LCCN 2023048888 (ebook) | ISBN
   9781493081080 (cloth) | ISBN 9781493081097 (ebook)
Subjects: LCSH: Mansfield, Pincus, 1924–2019. | World War,
   1939–1945—Aerial operations, American. | United States. Army Air
   Forces—Aerial gunners—Biography. | United States. Army Air Forces
   Bombardment Group (Heavy), 453rd—Biography. | World War,
   1939–1945—Campaigns—Western Front. | United States. Army Air
   Forces—Military life.
Classification: LCC D790.253 453rd M36 2024  (print) | LCC D790.253 453rd
   (ebook) | DDC 940.544973092 [B]—dc23/eng/20231026
LC record available at https://lccn.loc.gov/2023048887
LC ebook record available at https://lccn.loc.gov/2023048888

♾ᵀᴹ  The paper used in this publication meets the minimum requirements of American National
Standard for Information Sciences—Permanence of Paper for Printed Library Materials, ANSI/
NISO Z39.48-1992.

*To my nephew Scott,*
*for asking the right questions.*
*Keep asking.*

*Lindy! Lindy!*
*Come on down!*
*Lindy! Lindy!*

—CHILDREN ON THE STREETS OF NEW YORK CITY
WHEN THEY SAW THE RARE AIRPLANE

# CONTENTS

# INTRODUCTION
## Target for Tonight

I DISCOVERED MY FATHER'S WAR TWICE. THE FIRST TIME AT AN EIGH-teenth-century pub in Wales and the second, back home, in a dresser drawer, a year before he died. Neither time was I looking for his war, or anything to do with World War II. Nor was I burning to know about his earlier life. Growing up I had heard about his boyhood and knew and liked his boyhood buddies. They were still his friends. But his story came and found me in bits and pieces, in the few things he had said, and in the many things he hadn't said. His war years were both absent and present, so incomplete that it would take me years to even find the outline.

My first hint came on a walking trip in Wales in my late twenties. I was walking the long path that ran along the border with England, following, in part, King Offa's eighth-century border-defending earthen bank. The countryside was spectacular. The path took me to valleys of sheep in lambing time, fields of bluebells along the River Wye, Tintern Abbey, and small, one-pub villages.

One afternoon I came off the path to the Powis Arms, a Georgian era pub and inn, a place listing and askew as if the centuries were a rough sea. It is surprising how much wood can sag and lean over a few centuries. There's wasn't a straight line in the place. When you put down your pint glass, it listed at least 10 degrees.

At the bar in the pub, I was chatting with a fellow who, it turned out, was there because the flying club from the Severn Valley was meeting. We got to talking—as the only American, I'm sure I stood out. In the course of talking about flying I told him that my father had flown in the war, in a bomber, a B-24.

Say no more. He bought me a pint and invited me to their meeting, fairly insisted upon it, as much as an Englishman would tell a stranger what to do. They were watching a famous film about the war that night. I really should see it. At the meeting, I was introduced as an honored guest. My father—with an assist from 350,000 others in the Eighth Air Force—had helped to win the war.

The film, *Target for Tonight*, was like no other World War II movie I'd ever seen. It was made in one of the war's most uncertain hours—1941, when Great Britain was alone, having just dodged the threat of a Nazi invasion. It's a quiet film, starkly underpopulated, rickety, dark, and infused with British politeness. The officers often say, "good morning" and "thank you" to one another when communicating key information. Even in wartime, manners count. The Royal Air Force's Bomber Command was a small operation of mostly men, talking on phones, giving terse, but polite orders, keeping track of the bombers that were out flying a mission on a two-story-tall chalkboard, as if they were recording scores from cricket matches around the country. The RAF's Film Production Unit used Bomber Command's headquarters with the actual officers speaking scripted lines and the crews of No. 149 Squadron, most of whom would be killed in the war. There's no swagger, no tough guys getting it done. No one barks orders or even raises his voice.

We only see one airplane, a two-engine bomber, a Wellington, and its crew of five. There are no big flying scenes—they flew at night so that would be challenging to film—no bombers in formations, no mass war. The biggest scene shows maybe twenty men at a briefing. This is the smallest war movie you're ever likely to see. *Target for Tonight* runs for only forty-seven minutes.

The flight of that bomber, *F for Freddie*, takes up most of the film. They hit their target—an oil depot on the Rhine. The first four bombs miss, but the fifth is a direct hit. We see the oil depot burning, but again it seems like a small fire, a campfire in the dark.

*F for Freddie* is hit by shrapnel. The radio man is wounded, left lying on the floor, and the port engine is damaged, losing oil pressure. They limp back, landing in a dense fog. The commanders worry them home, waiting long after the others have returned. The crew reports in to be debriefed, looking really rather fresh, and off they go. The last line is spoken by one of the two commanding officers: "Well old boy, how about some bacon and eggs?" and we see a short reprise of the burning depot.

If you think about the big Nazi propaganda films like *Triumph of the Will*, made in 1935, with its immense Nazi rally, this British film shrinks even more. *Target for Tonight* leaves almost the entire war to be sketched in by the viewer's imagination: skies filled with bombers, puffs of dark smoke from the anti-aircraft guns, the Luftwaffe's Messerschmitts diving to attack, air raid sirens and burning cities on the home front, the battles on the ground, Hitler and Churchill. This may give the film its power. But what came across to me was how relentless the bomber war was. Hours of planning and preparation, followed by hours in the air, and then a return to do it all again. It was grinding and grim. And it was industrial. The production of destruction, the job of destroying your enemy, was a routine grind.

I left the inn the next morning after a terrible night of sleep—there were pigeons or rats scratching in the twisted, leaning walls all around me. But I would carry *Target for Tonight* with me for years. I knew then that my father, as a teenager, had joined a wartime routine that was something like this.

In that film, the war's fury is hidden. In 1941 Britain, no one needed to be reminded of what they were up against. But in the years since, we've hidden from ourselves the cataclysm and horror of a world at war. The commemorations and retellings of World War II became part of our forgetting. Some part of that forgetting was necessary for the men who fought, otherwise how could they come home, how could they find peace?

And there I left the war, but it kept finding me. Writing about the spirit that moves us to preserve and restore all manner of old things, I examined buildings, neighborhoods, landscapes, machinery, and endangered animals and ecosystems. I also wrote about our newest antique—aviation.

At their birth in the years before World War I, airplanes were the most exciting thing anyone had ever seen. Crowds filled fairgrounds to watch them fly by and then rushed to the aviator once he landed, at times carrying him away on their shoulders. If an airplane flew over a city, people raced to the rooftops and hung out the windows just to catch a glimpse, to see for themselves that it was really true: "Man," as it was said then, "could fly like the birds." They climbed trees, ladders, chimneys, anything to get closer. Men waved their hats, women their handkerchiefs. "Many persons dance when they see an aeroplane in flight," said *The New York Tribune* in 1911 when the first aviator flew over Manhattan. Think of the wonders that awaited. But in just a few years, people would be running away from airplanes as they dove to kill them, as they did on a market day in Guernica, Spain, on April 26, 1937. Soon they'd be hiding in bomb shelters as their city was destroyed. "All inventions grow up and go to war. Airplanes become weapons. That's the heartbreak," I wrote in *The Same Ax, Twice: Restoration and Renewal in a Throwaway Age.*

Ten years later, writing about our love of home and our efforts to create home, I wrote about the three most profound insights into the essence of what it means to dwell, to be at home on the earth, written by three philosophers—German, French, and Swiss—in the ruins of Europe's civilization after World War II. They were trying to find their way home through the rubble.

"Destroyed" was the most frequently used adjective in Europe just after the war, said historian Mario Praz. "Wherever you looked, you could see only shattered, ruined buildings, the hollow orbits of windows, and fragments of walls, houses split in two, with the pathetic sight of some still-furnished corner, dangling above the rubble, surrounded by ruin: pictures hanging on broken walls, a kitchen with the pots still on the stove." The ruins are our "reality," said Hans Werner Richter in 1947. "They are the outer symbol of the inner insecurity of the people of our age. The ruins live in us as we in them." Close to half of the housing in Germany had been destroyed or damaged. One in five English dwellings had been "affected by bombings."

"The twentieth century was the century of the burning house. More houses were set afire in war than at any other time in history. Great advances were made in bombing and burning houses. A house could be smashed by high explosive bombs. It could be set ablaze by various mixes of gasoline, napalm, magnesium, and thermite. It could be vaporized by the splitting of an atom," I wrote in *Dwelling in Possibility: Searching for the Soul of Shelter.*

I vowed to never write another word about World War II, but almost ten years on, I received an unexpected inheritance. It was not a fortune; it was a riddle. My father, Pincus Mansfield, like most men of his generation, refused to talk about the war. It was a rule with him and millions of other men. He had said a few things about his time in England, but nothing ever about combat.

In his last years, he was living alone and enjoying it, but worrying the hell out of all of us, even with his daytime helpers. So, we convinced him to go to a nursing home, a veteran's home as it turned out. We began to clean out the old house. He and my mother had moved in when it was new in 1955. It was the only house our family had lived in. Needless to say there was a lot of stuff, layers of time and memories mixed in among the too-muchness of every little thing.

Cleaning up one day, in a small drawer with his cufflinks and tie clips, I found some small, unlined, pocket-sized notebook pages, folded over and tossed aside, sitting as they had for almost sixty-five years. It was an account of each bomber mission he had flown as he had recorded it when he was nineteen and twenty years old. I had no idea such a record even existed. I quickly read through it, drank it down in a gulp. Some of the missions he flew were harrowing, marked by attacking fighters, anti-aircraft cannon blowing holes in his plane, and wounding crewmen. I began to fill in the details, helped by miles of microfilmed records of the Army Air Forces, and the memories he had recorded in his last years of growing up, and training for the war, memories that always stopped well short of what had happened in the air at war. I began to undo the forgetting as best I could.

# 1

# "YOUR WINGS ARE WAITING"

At age 18, out of high school already for more than two years, my father volunteered for the Army Air Forces. He had been drafted, but they did not take him. He had only one good hand. Men with lesser physical problems were turned away. (Thirty percent of draftees were classified 4-F.) But he returned, maybe more than once, and convinced the Air Force that they couldn't fly without him. He was inducted on August 13, 1943. He would be trained to be a waist gunner, one of the men shooting a machine gun out of the open "gun port" window of the B-24 Liberator bomber.

The news that he would be leaving for the Air Force hit his family hard. "My parents thought I was nuts and did until their dying day," he said. His Uncle Sammy bought him a trumpet at a hock shop. "Here, when they hear you play maybe they won't send you overseas," he said. He didn't think his one-handed nephew was going to win the war.

The trumpet had gotten him out of high school. "I graduated by the skin of my teeth," he said. The two credits he had for playing with a borrowed instrument in Senior Band gave him just enough to graduate. He played in the band at football games. When they brought the injured players off by the bandstand "you could hear the poor kids moaning."

He loved music. With his good friend and fellow band member, Larry, he'd gone to Carnegie Hall to see Paul Whiteman conduct Gershwin's *Rhapsody in Blue*. "Whiteman's name was all over the newspapers," he recalled. They bought tickets for the highest balcony, and there sitting in the front, they leaned forward, rested on their folded arms, "drinking in the music."

He had excelled in grammar school, particularly in math, and was advanced one grade. "This, of course, turned out to be a mistake," he said, because he was always the youngest and smallest kid in his class. "But I overcame it, I think."

He was a numbers guy, a born engineer. In English class at James Monroe High School, he sat by the window watching them build the Bronx-Whitestone Bridge. They built the bridge out from each shore. "I often wondered what if they joined the two halves and they don't match?" Longfellow may have gone right by in that English class, but he had the right engineering question.

The morning he went off to war, his mother took him to the train. She was crying. She may have thought she was sending her only son to his death. There was a song he used to hear her singing as she cleaned house, "I Didn't Raise My Boy to Be a Soldier," a popular song from World War I:

> Ten million soldiers to the war have gone,
> Who may never return again.
> Ten million mother's hearts must break
> For the ones who died in vain. . . .
> It's time to lay the sword and gun away,
> There'd be no war today,
> If mother's all would say,
> I didn't raise my boy to be a soldier.

"It didn't mean anything to me, of course," he said. He got on the train.

His parents were immigrants from the same Lithuanian shtetl. They both spoke Yiddish and English, so they were not isolated by language, but first-generation American children have to complete the crossing. It's left to them to figure out how to be American. For an American boy in the 1930s that meant cowboy movies, radio shows, playing ball in the street, and flying model airplanes. (He was in the model airplane club in high school.) Playing in the street when they saw a plane flying over they called out *Lindy! Lindy! Come on down!*

"My cousin Harold lived a few blocks away," he recalled. "He and I palled around. We used to go to movies together on Shabbas"—the Sabbath—"This was frowned upon by our parents, but we would sneak out and go see a Western, that's about all they had at the show. Ken Maynard was the star cowboy. My personal preference was Hoot Gibson. He would spin a lasso and dance in the middle of it. I really liked him. Ken Maynard was the hero to the girls." In one movie, cowboy Maynard or cowboy Gibson climbed up on some rocks and they could see he was wearing sneakers. Even a Bronx kid knew that cowboys didn't wear sneakers.

A Bronx boyhood.

Radio was a new thing back when my father was learning to read and walking to school by himself. "We passed by a brand-new store that opened up. The sign on the window said, 'R-A-D-One-Oh,' or, 'Rad-Ten.' I didn't realize till later it said 'Radio.' It had just come out, and he was advertising the radio. My father and mother bought one and brought it into the house."

He liked listening to *Og, Son of Fire*—about a kid in the stone age—*Famous Jury Trials, Hollywood Hotel, The Lone Ranger, 20,000 Years in Sing Sing, Let's Pretend, Little Orphan Annie, Bobby Benson*—he grew up on a ranch with cowboys—and *Buck Rogers in the 25th Century*. We'd talk about these shows when I called, and I'd Google the show. I'd never heard of many of them. He liked this game of Google-me-the-past. He was amazed at how quickly you could find out about something. He never owned a computer and had never been online.

They also listened to prize fights, some of which were red-hot, front-page confrontations between Italians and Jews, Blacks and whites. The aftermath of Max Baer beating Primo Carnera for the Heavyweight Championship caused such an uproar in his fourth grade English class that Mrs. Marla, the teacher, gave a boy three cents to go buy *The Daily News*, which they then took turns reading aloud in class. The Italian kids thought that Carnera had been cheated out of his title by Baer, who was Jewish, and wore a Star of David on his boxing trunks.

My father wasn't too interested in baseball—he didn't know the game. In the early 1930s, the three New York teams, seeing radio as a rival, refused to broadcast their games. He did play stickball in the street with a broomstick for a bat and a rubber ball, the game stripped down to hitting and running around until someone caught the ball. The sewer drains, every couple of hundred feet apart, defined the game. "We used to say if you could hit three sewers, you're really a champ."

His sister Sylvia would sit in front of the radio and write down the lyrics to any song in shorthand. "I didn't realize at the time that it wasn't a hobby with her. She was studying for a shorthand test. My sister was five years older than I am. We got along pretty good as brother and sister. That's a pretty large age gap for children, but we managed." She would soon be making more than their father.

"We also had a Victrola, or what you would call today a record player. My father took a particular liking to a record of a young lady by the name of Helen Morgan. She would sing songs from *Show Boat*, which had been recorded recently. He'd play it over and over again. He'd play some Yiddish records, too."

His father, Elai, worked in the "needle trades" as a milliner, a hat maker. As his father's work rose and fell, they changed neighborhoods. When times were good they lived near the Grand Concourse, and when work dried up in the Great Depression they moved to a rough neighborhood, where his father opened the first of two luncheonettes, little corner stores that sold a few items and had a counter to serve food. His mother, Ida, ran the store when his father had more work.

Cash was scarce. Customers bought cigarettes one at a time for a penny and they bought them on credit. They couldn't afford a pack. They "trusted" for the cigarettes, they said, "going on the book." They'd come in on payday and settle bills totaling thirteen or twenty-five cents. They also made a little money from a rented pinball machine. When Fiorello LaGuardia was mayor in 1942 they lost that small bit of income. Police were raiding shops to seize illegal pinball machines. LaGuardia thought the "evil contraptions" were "insidious nickel stealers" luring children into gambling. The police confiscated thousands of machines. LaGuardia was photographed smashing the machines with a sledgehammer. They were dumped at sea. Elai was tipped off, though. He locked the pinball machine in the bathroom and convinced the police not to look in there, saying a boy rumored to have VD had just been in there. The cops washed their hands and left. He got rid of the pinball machine.

People came into the apartment courtyard where all the laundry hung on lines, singing for pennies and looking for clothes they could sell. "We'd throw pennies out the window to the street singers. Then there'd be people who'd come around and yell up into the tenements, 'Buy cash clothes. Buy cash clothes.'"

They weren't "comfortable," as they said then, but they weren't wanting, either. Each summer they went away with two families they knew to "the mountains" in upstate New York. A farmer rented them bungalows, known as *kuch aleyns* in Yiddish, "cook for yourself." In the early 1930s,

5

when an aunt and uncle and their two children hit hard times, they took in their family, crowding their modest apartment.

In his last years he was recording these memories on a tape recorder we had given him and sending me the tapes. He portrays himself as a good kid, a straight arrow, which I'm sure is true. He talks about guys he knew in the Air Force who could break the rules, go AWOL and never get caught. They could get away with anything. "That's something I could never do."

"I remember living on Clinton Avenue. I didn't particularly get along with the other boys," he said. "They called me all sorts of dirty names and made fun of the fact that one of my hands was slightly deformed. My mother used to lecture me before I went out to play. She would say, 'If you get into a fight, make sure you give back.'"

I missed this the first time I listened to one of his tapes. His memories were almost all happy, one of those New York City boyhoods that was long ago seized by the nostalgia machine and preserved in sepia. But this story had gone right by me. Of course kids would have been cruel and taunt him about his hand. I had never thought of that. He had a seriously malformed left hand from a birth defect. His hand, when I saw it, was big, round, and club-like, with a separate thumb, almost like a fleshy boxing glove. It never stopped him from anything—dating beautiful women, flying, working as a draftsman, building furniture and new walls in the unfinished basement, or fixing the car.

When I grew up, his bad hand was invisible to me. I never noticed it, thought it odd, or thought anything about it until a specific moment I remember well. I was five or six, maybe, playing with the boy next door. We were running about in the fields that began just beyond our backyards. I remember the exact spot just at the corner of our backyard by the small cherry tree, where he asked me, "What happened to your dad's hand?"

"Whaddya' mean?" I probably said.

"What's wrong with it?"

"I dunno."

6

After he graduated from high school early at age sixteen and a half, he was pretty miserable. There was no going to college—there was no money for it and his grades weren't good enough. He was studying engineering—"Aero Drafting"—in night school and working part-time in his family's luncheonette.

To cheer him up, his mother bought him a portable radio—a heavy thing weighing nearly ten pounds; batteries were heavy then and the radio had tubes. He'd sit in the park and listen to it or carry it around. "I was this kid walking around the Bronx with a big radio," he said. They had to buy it "on time," something that his father was strictly against, so they didn't tell him. Each week my father went and paid twenty-five cents on the radio. He was lonely that fall. Most of his friends were still in school.

He did have a close circle of friends. They called themselves the "Five Guys from the Bronx." He was the youngest. He doesn't present himself as having any special abilities, but the others did, as he tells it: Harold could build anything; Hy was a super salesman; Larry could pick up any instrument and in a few minutes be playing a tune; and Harold's older brother, Charlie, who didn't graduate from high school, never stopped educating himself. He always had piles of books with him. "Any time he found a word he didn't know, he looked it up and wrote it on a thick pad." He taught himself about opera and ballet. Charlie looked after him like he was his little brother, and Ida, my father's mother, looked after Charlie and Harold like they were her own.

They all went to war. Harold first to the Navy, Hy to Papua New Guinea, Larry to the Army, my father and Charlie to the Air Force. Harold loved the wide-open Pacific. At night he'd sit on the fantail, smoking and thinking about things under a big sky of stars. Hy suffered in the tropical jungles. He was scorched by the sun and lost so much weight from being sick that his mother had trouble picking him out in a photo he sent home. Larry was taken to witness one of the A-bomb blasts in the Pacific just after the war. Charlie was badly wounded on a bombing mission, flying after he had completed his full tour. They had asked to him stay. My father visited him in the hospital. He was shocked to see

7

that Charlie was far worse off than he'd first let on. My father was crying when he left. Charlie was all cut up and had only a fifty-fifty chance of living, but he made it.

The Army Air Forces claimed that it only took the fittest men. "They must be a very special kind of young men. They must, in fact, be the best physical and mental specimens the country produces," the novelist John Steinbeck wrote for the Air Force one year before they took my father. "He must be very healthy, and he must have no physical disability of any kind."

Why would they take a one-handed eighteen-year-old? The short answer is that in 1943, when he joined, they were losing the war. They were losing 75 percent of the men they trained and sent into battle. The Air Force had decided that flying twenty-five missions in a "heavy bomber" like the B-24 or the B-17 Flying Fortress was a full combat tour, but this was wishful thinking. In 1943, only 25 percent of their fliers completed 25 missions. The rest were shot down, killed in action, missing in action, or prisoners. For 75 percent of the young aviators in 1943, their war ended with an acronym: KIA, MIA, POW. During most of the war—until the Battle of the Bulge in December 1944—Germany held more POWs from the Air Force than from the infantry. Before the Allies landed in Italy in September 1943, the Air Force was the only way they could fight on the Continent.

On each mission, each raid to bomb factories, railroads, and airfields, they lost, on average, five percent of their airmen. The math is simple and stark: in twenty-five missions they were going to lose everybody—and 25 percent of the replacements. "It was like a death in the family every time a crew returned and found that friends in another B-17 or B-24 hadn't made it," said Andy Rooney, who as a sergeant was a reporter for the Army newspaper, *Stars & Stripes*. Empty cots sat with photos of the waiting wives, girlfriends, and mothers. Early in 1943, a bomber crewman's average life expectancy was fifteen missions. On the British side, only 17 percent of Bomber Command's crews could be expected to fly their required thirty missions. It was, some said, like playing Russian Roulette, but with worse odds.

The Eighth Air Force had more "fatal causalities"—twenty-six thousand—than the entire Marine Corps. By the war's end, ten thousand bombers had been lost. The Air Force's war planners, known as the "Bomber Mafia," had thought they might lose three hundred bombers in the entire war. Only Pacific submarine crews suffered a higher fatality rate.

Navigator Lou Bober, an insurance actuary, knew a mortality table when he saw one. He told his pilot, "Skipper, mathematically there just ain't any way we're gonna live through this thing." Somehow, he survived to fly his full tour.

"By the end of 1943, the entire Allied strategic bombing effort was in danger of collapse," says historian Tami Davis Biddle. In one week in October, which came to be called "Black Week"—from October 8th to the 14th, in four missions, the Eighth Air Force lost 148 bombers. On one mission over Munster on October 10, one bomb group, the 100th, sent thirteen B-17s into Germany. Twelve were shot down over the target in seven minutes. The lone survivor, *Rosie's Riveters*, returned flying on two of its four engines with a big hole in one wing and many smaller ones in the fuselage.

Some of the worst losses of the early war were taken in the raid on the ball bearing factories in Schweinfurt on "Black Thursday," October 14, 1943. Sixty bombers were lost and six hundred men were killed or captured. (Headline: *600 Airmen Lost Over Schweinfurt.*) More than 120 returning planes were damaged. Seventeen were scrapped. Only thirty-three bombers out of a force of 229 landed without battle damage.

"The fighters were unrelenting; it was simply murder," said First Lt. Carl Abele, a navigator on the B-17 *Blackjack.* "We were being mauled," said Sgt. Eugene T. Carson, a nineteen-year-old tail gunner on the B-17 *Tiger Girl.* "To our rear and off to one side a B-17 took a direct hit. A wing came off and the airplane went into a flat spin. Although I knew my plea was without meaning and could not be heard, I found myself urging the crew to get out.

"We dropped our bombs and turned for home. The intercom was a constant chatter as the crew called out Luftwaffe fighter locations." They

9

crossed into Belgium looking for their escort fighters. "They were not to be seen. Our escort was weathered in, still on the ground in England," said Carson. "I could not see how we were going to make it home." When they reached the Channel, the Luftwaffe fell away. "I bent forward, rested my head on the window and began to shake and cry uncontrollably. I stopped long enough to take a deep breath and say, "Thank you, God.'"

Of the bombers that made it to Germany, 30 percent were lost; more than 18 percent of the airmen were killed, wounded, or missing. Morale plummeted; men talked of not flying again. Ball bearing production was only halted for six weeks. The Nazis reorganized the industry, protecting it from concentrated attack. The Air Force learned that they needed to build escort fighter planes to defend the bombers all the way to the target.

The losses that fall depleted the Eighth Air Force. They wouldn't fly deep into Germany in clear weather for the rest of the year. The Luftwaffe controlled the sky.

The winter of 1943, as the Air Force was just entering the fight, had been bleak. "The mud was atmosphere. You breathed it in even if you didn't want to, it was under your nails, it was in the grooves of your hands," said Col. Curtis LeMay. Coal was in short supply; the food was bad. There were heavy causalities and low morale. LeMay's 305th BG (Bomb Group) had lost nearly half of its airmen.

"Bomber bases were damn depressing places to visit. Death was always in the air, even though the guys were trying hard to laugh and forget," said Andy Rooney. "Frequently a crew member would have dinner after a raid and then go back to his bunk and sit there, staring at nothing. Many of the bomber crews were always on the ragged edge of breaking down mentally. It was a combination of the fear of death and the relentlessness of the loss of friends."

Walter Cronkite cautioned his fellow reporter Eric Sevareid when he first took him to a bomber base, "Don't make friends with the kids. ...It's too much when they are lost, and most of them, you know, will be." And *United Press* reporter Harrison Salisbury said, "To fly in the Eighth Air Force then was to hold a ticket to a funeral. Your own."

One gunner, fresh from training in the states and ready for the war, was shaken by his first hours at his assigned airfield. "When I first got over there, we were in the chow line to eat, I looked at these guys and they looked like zombies. I said, 'Man, what is it with these guys?' They were scared."

The first men knew they were part of an experiment to learn how to fight an air war. They sometimes referred to themselves as "guinea pigs." "Is anyone scared?" the commander of the 367th BG, Col. Maurice Preston, asked his men. "If not, there's something wrong with you. I'll give you a little clue how to fight this war—make believe you're dead already; the rest comes easy."

The Air Force was desperate. They needed to train two crews for each one they lost. And it wasn't just about replacing lost airmen. The Eighth Air Force was adding bomber crews so it could triple in size in 1944. The Air Force needed replacements. They needed an eighteen-year-old Bronx boy with only one good hand.

This grim portrait is not what they were hearing on the "home front." My father didn't think he had won a ticket to his own funeral.

Among the cowboy movies at the Fox Crotona Theatre, a vast 2,500-seat survivor from the silent era, he probably saw a short film by the Oscar-winning star of *The Philadelphia Story*. In one scene, Jimmy Stewart addresses a "fellow who works in a filling station," a would-be recruit, and with that side-slipping Northern drawl, he says, "From where I'm standing, you look like you're about to sprout wings." Stewart was recruiting for his new employer, the Army Air Forces.

"This war we're fighting today and tomorrow and the next day until we win is a war of the air. The whole world knows that," he says. He talks about the excitement of flying, the good pay, and winning the attention of girls. "You find out the effect those shiny little wings have on a gal and it's phenomenal," he says as we watch a woman walk away from an Army officer she's been dancing with when an Air Force pilot walks in. "The Army Air Forces need 15,000 captains, 40,000 lieutenants, 35,000 flying sergeants. How about it?" Stewart asks, neglecting to say that most of those signing up would serve as gunners, and that thousands more wouldn't fly—they were needed for the ground crews. Those positions were briefly noted later in the film. All the glamour is showcased.

As airplanes dive and fly past, one after another, Stewart says, "So listen to the roar of those motors, young men of America, and heed their call. Soon the skies will be filled with the greatest air armada the world has ever seen. Our American Army Air Forces. The best planes ever built. . . . That's why we'll lick the Axis."

Facing the camera, Stewart closes his sales pitch: "Now this is your place. This is where you'll serve America best. Young men of America, your future's in the sky. Your wings are waiting." Stewart's film, *Winning Your Wings*, was important in recruiting 100,000 men, said General H. "Hap" Arnold, Chief of the Army Air Forces.

The young men of America wanted to fly. They signed up because of *Lindy!* Airplanes were the celebrity technology of the era. They were what made today different from yesterday. Aloft they'd be free from the tedium of their parents' jobs—if they still had jobs—in the factory, the farm, the office, or the corner store. In the air there are no factories and farms, no family businesses, no time clock. Simple as that. Flying was thrilling; flying was freedom. They wanted wings.

My father's first stop was every enlistee's first stop, basic training—boot camp. He was sent to Miami Beach.

At physical training,

> *the instructor got up on a platform and he said, "I'm gonna demonstrate to you Jujitsu—Jujitsu is a Japanese defense. If you know how to do it, you can use your opponent's weight to overcome him. And Judo is the same thing, only, with a little change in maneuvers, you could kill a man with Judo. And I'll teach you both."*
>
> *So, we all lined up. He demonstrated Jujitsu on the platform, and it looked so easy. I lined up in front of my opponent, a rather stout young man. He outweighed me by at least twenty, maybe thirty*

*pounds. The instructor yells out,* Attack! *So, he came toward me, and I grabbed his hand and I couldn't move him. It was like holding onto a stone because he was so heavy. That didn't go too well.*

The rest of the eight weeks was taken up by "The School of the Soldier"—"military discipline, customs, and courtesies"; medical aid; marksmanship; camouflage; defense against chemical attack; close order drills; night operations. There were many days of marching, bivouacs, drills, and training on the obstacle course, climbing ropes, pulling yourself over slanted walls, balancing on planks, moving hand-to-hand hanging from horizontal ladders or poles, vaulting low fences, and crawling with your rifle under barbed wire and through narrow tunnels.

With only one good hand, I don't know how he did his training, including the most basic pushups, pull-ups, and squat thrusts, let alone climbing and crawling his way through the obstacle course. I don't know how much he could do with his bad left hand, but I know that it stood out.

He was out in the sun all day. "I sustained a severe case of sunburn," he said. They treated him with Lubricane, which he used for years after. It was always in the medicine cabinet. "As soon it touches you, the burn disappears. It really works."

"It was quite hot there in Miami Beach. They gave me a salt pill; why, I don't know. They just said you have to take it. So, I took the salt pill. Maybe fifteen, twenty minutes later, I threw up my guts. I couldn't handle it. And that was Basic Training."

As they marched around in the heat carrying heavy packs, they passed hotels with signs that said, "No Jews," "Gentiles Only," and "Restricted Clientele." This left him with a life-long aversion to Florida. I asked him once if it was hard being Jewish in the Army. "I had a couple of skirmishes," he answered. "Nothing serious; nothing to talk about."

He wasn't done with Florida. He was sent north to Tyndall Field in the Florida panhandle.

## "Here Is Your Gun"

After basic training, he met his gun—"the Caliber .50 Browning Machine Gun M2 Aircraft, Basic." The .50 cal. Browning is almost eternal, used in every war from the 1930s through World War II, Korea, Vietnam, the Gulf Wars, and Afghanistan. He wasn't looking for a gun; he was looking for an airplane and this was true of almost everyone in gunnery school. Some of the trainees were disappointed. They had volunteered hoping to become flying aces with the kills marked under the cockpit of their fighters. They were "air-minded," as they said then, plane crazy, a generation desperate to fly. The aviator was the glamour boy, the headline hero, the colossus who flew out of the Jazz Age and right over the Great Depression. At gunnery school, the enlistees wanted to be Lindy or Jimmy Doolittle or Wiley Post or a squadron of other headline hero aviators whose names have now faded. They wanted to fly, not shoot guns all day in the heat of the Deep South. The wash-out rate was usually under 10 percent, but some classes hit 20 percent. They were sent on to other assignments.

The Air Force labored to make their recruits care about guns. Gunnery school was about the Browning and other guns 'round the clock, about knowing the .30 cal. and .50 cal. machine gun "better than its mother does," as one training film said.

"Your job is to become enough of a machine gun expert to use and care for the gun properly and to make emergency repairs—so that no attacking fighter will ever catch you unable to fight back," said the training manual, which sought to impress the recruits.

> *Your gun fires 750 to 850 shots a minute—fourteen shots a second. The bullets, weighing nearly two ounces each, leave the barrel at 1,977 miles an hour—2,900 feet a second. This speed is called the muzzle velocity. Even at a distance of four miles—the gun's maximum range—one of those bullets will kill a man. At closer distances, the bullets wreck anything that gets in the way.*

They had to know the 150 working parts of the Browning so well that they could take it apart and put it back together while they were blindfolded. The instructor stood over them and barked,

*You will now assemble the gun. In doing so, you are to change the direction of feed to feed from the right. And make all necessary adjustments. In addition, I have put in three parts that are broken. You must find these broken parts before you actually put them in their proper places in the groups; hand them to me and name them. You must follow the order of assembly of groups taught in the weapons course. Is this clear?*

The blindfold test stood between the would-be airmen and getting airborne. They had to pass this test to go on to the shooting ranges on the ground and in the air. This kind of mechanical problem played to my father's strengths. I'm sure he had his gun apart and reassembled without trouble. Growing up, this test was one of the only things about the Army he mentioned. I remember seeing the manual for the Browning Machine Gun in among our books, mixed in with the Book-of-the-Month Club hardcovers, a thin tan paperback with a textured cover. Other than his uniform tunic, which hung under the stairs in the basement, growing moldy, this was the only sign of his wartime service in our house.

The Air Force wanted the public to believe that a legion of sharpshooters was streaming into its gunnery schools, which after a six-week course, would make them ready to topple the Axis. They would be "the executioners of the air."

The best aerial gunner had an early start, said John Steinbeck in a book he was hired by the Air Force to write. "The ideal gunner" began as a little boy shooting rubber-tipped arrows, moved to BB guns and by age nine he "ranged the hills and the woods hunting squirrels" on his own with a .22, so that "the pointing of a gun was as natural as the pointing of his finger." At age twelve, given his first shotgun, he learned to "lead the target," ducks, quail, and grouse. He knew not to aim where they were, but where they were headed. Shooting a duck from the sky midflight, Steinbeck claimed, was the same as knocking down Zeros, Stukas, and Henkels. Hunting was the defining background experience. "One does not really learn to shoot a rifle or a machine gun in a few weeks," said Steinbeck.

The gunnery schools were full of these "gun-minded young men" who the Air Force was turning into aerial gunners of "deadly accuracy," he reassured his readers—the mothers and fathers of recruits, and the future recruits. There are "already Paul Bunyons among our gunners," he wrote. But there wasn't a legion of native marksmen. The gunnery schools were graduating thousands of men a week. If they had all been squirrel hunters, the country would have been squirrel-free. Most men, including my father, had never fired a shot.

The Air Force was building seven gunnery schools in haste. The curriculum wasn't ready. At the war's start there were no specialized gunnery schools—and scarcely an air force. In 1938, after Hitler had annexed Austria and taken part of Czechoslovakia, the Army Air Corps only had 1,200 airplanes, many of them obsolete, and 22,700 officers and enlisted men. The Air Corps ranked a dismal twentieth in the world, behind many smaller countries. The Luftwaffe was four times as large and growing fast. (And the entire U.S. Army was also far down the list, sixteenth in the world, trailing Romania.) Two years later, in May 1940, Congress gave General Arnold, head of the Air Corps, a staggering sum. "In forty-five minutes, I was given $1.5 billion and told to get an air force," said Arnold.

The instructors were still figuring out what they would teach when the first students began to arrive. They had to teach the new recruits how to hit a moving target while firing from a moving airplane. No one really knew how to teach that.

Tyndall Field was one of the first to open. The airfield was near Panama City on the Florida panhandle, alone on its own Gulf Coast peninsula. The first staff moved in, by chance, on December 7, 1941, the day Pearl Harbor was attacked.

My father arrived at Tyndall Field in March 1944, joining Flexible Gunnery Class 44-8, Sections 27 and 28. Flexible guns swiveled on mounts or were in moving gun turrets. Fixed guns were in an airplane's nose and wings. The flexible gun is what you see in war movies when a gunner is pivoting his machine gun as if he were slicing open the sky.

His six-week course began with meeting his gun and learning ballistics—the path of a bullet—and gun mounts and turrets, gun sights and sighting targets, aircraft recognition, shooting a machine gun without overheating the barrel, hours of tests and physical training.

Once they had rebuilt the Browning machine gun blindfolded, students began at the BB gun range, firing a fixed .22 cal. gun at a fixed target. Firing at moving targets on the skeet ranges was next. At the Moving Base Range, they fired from a turret mounted on a truck as it drove at 15 to 25 mph around a triangular track. Clay pigeons were launched at different trajectories from thirty-foot towers around the track. At the Moving Target Range or Jeep Range, students placed around the track and fired a .22 cal. machine gun at targets pulled by a remote-controlled jeep. Students enjoyed missing the target and hitting the jeep.

The ground ranges took a great deal of time to set up and score, and they used up a lot of ammunition. In 1943, at Tyndall alone, the ammunition they expended was equivalent to 17 percent of all the rounds fired in combat by the Air Force in the entire war. In their two last weeks, the students finally got into airplanes to fire at banners towed by other planes. This, too, was cumbersome and slow. Only a few students could go up at a time, each firing a bullet painted a different color. Once the banners were dropped on the ground, it took instructors a long time to score the results. Students were hindered by pilots who, weary of the tedium of flying straight and level, "engaged in mild acrobatics to relieve the boredom of the routine, thus effectively terrorizing and otherwise incapacitating many a green student," said one study.

The schools tried different "synthetic trainers" to increase training time. At Tyndall they used the Spotlight Trainer, a shed where the student gunner practiced aiming at a spotlight; the Waller Trainer, which had the gunner "shooting" at targets placed before a panoramic movie scene; and the 3A-2 Trainer, called the "Jam Handy," which projected actual combat films taken from different gun positions on a bomber. These training aids were in short supply, had many limitations, and yielded mixed results.

To reach a generation that had grown up at the movies, the schools used a new thing—training films—including *The Rear Gunner* with Lt.

Ronald Reagan as a pilot and Lt. Burgess Meredith as the tail gunner who goes through training. As the title is spelled out in bullet holes tearing into an airplane's fuselage, an energetic men's chorus sings the Air Force song: "Off We Go into the Wild Sky Yonder." I'd heard that song—we all probably have. (The first line was later changed to "the wild *blue* yonder.") But I'd never heard the last verse, sung as the bullet holes are still chewing up an airplane: *If you'd live to be a gray-haired wonder / keep the nose out of the blue!* This song was only four years old at the time, having been chosen by a committee of Air Force wives who may have seen some truth in lines like *We live in fame or go down in flame.*

The film follows the new tail gunner through training. An officer welcomes a classroom of new arrivals, "embryo marksmen of the sky:" "Your government is aware of the importance of flexible gunners in the victorious pursuit of this war. They know that the fire from your guns is the fire of freedom. Good luck. Aim well and shoot straight." At the film's end, the narrator rallies the troops by saying, "You gunners are the modern knights of fire, the administrators of life and death, an integral part of the greatest All-American team." Another training film, this one with a tough-talking instructor, was blunt: "This is what you are here for. To fire guns. To kill."

Gunnery training was, by unanimous consent, "the Army Air Forces' weakest training program," said one historian. The training was "inadequate," said a secret wartime Air Force study. Every aspect of teaching men to shoot from airplanes was debated and dismissed: whether skeet shooting did anything but teach skeet shooting (it wasn't anything like combat), or shooting from one airplane at a cloth target towed by another airplane (of "negligible" value—"No enemy fighter pilot would fly next to a bomber and let the gunners shoot at him"), or shooting from a moving truck (ineffective), or using simulators (again, it was nothing like the panicked moment when a fighter was closing in, with your life on the line).

The Air Force knew it had to simplify its training. There could be twelve different combinations of sights and turrets on a B-24. One single position might require four different training courses. Men were frequently assigned to turrets they hadn't trained on. Late in the war there were twenty different training courses in the gunnery schools. Officers didn't even agree about when a gunner should open fire at attacking fighters. At twelve-hundred yards? Six hundred yards? (Yes, six hundred, they decided.)

Students were not "retaining" their training. Gunners in the field failed tests that gunners in training passed. They didn't know targeting, maintenance, or how to strip a gun. Too often they had no experience operating guns in the air. Seventy percent of gunners in one survey had no training in the aircraft they were assigned to for combat. They had a "hopeless unfamiliarity with equipment," reported the Seventh Air Force in the Pacific.

Commanders at the front sent urgent pleas for better gunners. Their bombers were getting shot out of the sky. To improve training, in June 1943, the Air Force sent eighteen of their "key officers" in gunnery to study the war in Europe. Six were shot down.

Every part of the curriculum was altered and the hours of instruction nearly doubled. Students spent less time learning ballistic theory and the nomenclature of parts of the gun, and less time at something called the Malfunction Firing Range trying to figure out why a gun had jammed. At least fourteen different types of "synthetic trainers" were built, sixteen types of outdoor ranges, and five different practice missions were tried.

"Gun cameras" were set up to record "the aiming point" of an imaginary bullet. Before using the gun camera, fewer than 25 percent of trainees hit objects on the ground and not even 5 percent hit aerial targets, claimed the instructors at one school. After gun camera training, that inched up. With further training, the instructors claimed a hit rate near 60 percent. But gun cameras also failed review—gun camera scores were "subject to much error." And there was "little if any evidence of learning on gun camera missions."

Even aircraft identification was revamped. Students had formerly been taught an extensive system of looking at Wings, Engine, Fuselage and Tail (WEFT) to quickly—and it had to be quickly—identify an Fw 190 (theirs) from a P-47 (ours). It wasn't quick enough and was replaced by the more promising sounding "Flash system."

Teams of psychologists were dispatched to test for "machine gunner proficiency." They came up with a list of twenty "traits" that gunnery instructors valued, concluding that emotional control and motivation was "necessary." They prescribed aptitude tests for aerial gunners, running through sixty-two different tests, before the Aptitude Test for Aerial Gunners (AC30A) was given to one thousand G.I.s and discarded. (Steinbeck was closer with his squirrel-hunting nine-year-olds.)

The schools asked for more bombers and for fighters for training, for more ammunition, for more synthetic trainers. More of anything wouldn't have solved the fundamental problem: the Air Force could never specify the skills and training that would get more enemy planes shot down. The four-engine "heavy bombers"—the B-17 Flying Fortress and the B-24 Liberator—were armed with a half-dozen machine gun positions, but the gunner's role was oddly ambiguous. "The gunner was sometimes considered important, sometimes not; his contribution to the success of the mission sometimes crucial, sometimes inconsiderable," said a secret psychology study by the Air Force. Pilots were the stars; bombardiers and navigators were essential. Gunners were in limbo, maybe necessary, maybe not. The gunners themselves "seldom knew if they were good, poor, or indifferent." And yet by August 1944, the Air Force was graduating 3,500 gunners a week and would train nearly 300,000 before the war's end. They needed men, no matter how proficient they were.

The big problem was the obvious one: aiming the gun. On a bombing mission, the gunner, cold and on oxygen "after hours of inactivity . . . had to exercise split-second judgment." The gunner had to (1) Recognize the airplane—at six hundred yards the enemy would appear no bigger than a dime held at arm's length, edgewise. A glinting in the sky. (2) Estimate its distance. (The iron-ring gun sight made planes seem closer than they were. The plane's vibration also made accurate aiming difficult. The wind could be moving at 200 mph pressing on the gun.) (3) Estimate the difference in the speeds of his bomber and the enemy aircraft by "holding his sight stationary for one second." (4) "Compute the lead"—how far in front of the attacker to fire—by recalling a table he'd memorized. He had to aim where the attacking fighter was headed. He had to fire knowing the bullet would not go where the gun was pointing. Everything was in motion: two airplanes, and the gun itself. And: (5) Open fire. By that time, in combat, "there was usually no target in sight." That thin edge of a dime could appear and close upon a gunner so quickly that he could, at times, see the pilot's eyes, and then the fighter would be gone, all within three to six seconds. The rate of machine gun fire had increased somewhat between the wars, but aircraft speed had tripled. In the crowded seconds of an attack, only about 10 percent of gunners could open fire. It was a technological mismatch.

To explain all this, the Air Force called on Mel Blanc, the voice of Bugs Bunny, Daffy Duck, Porky Pig, and many others. In a black-and-white cartoon, *Position Firing*, Blanc's character, Trigger Joe, an Elmer Fudd-like B-17 waist gunner, learns how to use the gun sight's "rads" (radius) to shoot at the right spot in the sky after being shown the fighter's "pursuit curve" and a dizzying display of angles. Each angle of attack required moving the gun a different number of "rads." That was only the first judgment. "Your direction was right, but you had no correction for your deflection as the approach angle changed," the narrator tells Trigger Joe—The bomber pulls a just-fired bullet forward with it, deflecting its trajectory. Trigger Joe claims to get it by the end of the fourteen-minute-long film, but I'm still back at the first example of the paper boy throwing his newspaper at a porch long before he passes the house. I'm not alone. "The perceptual problem of estimating and setting off the appropriate rad leads was impressively difficult," the Air Force conceded.

They admitted that effective gunnery was elusive. Trigger Joe had a tough assignment. The confessions are all over the Air Force's studies: "The problem of the best manner of sighting a flexible gun was a continuous one." Firing in the air is "much more perplexing" than firing on the ground. "Even under optimum conditions" there was "a very small percentage of hits." Near the end of the war, the most effective gunnery on B-29s, which were a leap ahead of the older bombers, claimed to destroy only 4.2 percent of attacking fighters. Another 2.8 percent were "probably destroyed" and 5.1 percent were damaged. The gunner's job was to keep the enemy from coming too close; it was a defensive position.

Kills by gunners were not officially counted, unlike those for fighter pilots. And yet at the end of the war, the Air Force claimed that bombers had shot down more than six thousand airplanes in Europe, which was 80 percent of the number credited to fighters. From the training range to combat, the Air Force walked both sides of a contradiction: the gunner couldn't hit anything; the gunner was an unsung ace.

Ready, aim, fire, was the old military command. It had worked for Napoleon. But in the modern air war, every aspect of ready, aim, fire had to be reinvented. The Air Force did their best in six weeks of school but ended up sending their boys off to war after shooting at clay pigeons.

At gunnery school my father finally got to fly. He went up in a B-17. "My first thought was: 'Wow, this is just like the World's Fair.'" At the 1939 New York World's Fair, General Motors had engineered the fair's most popular attraction—a simulated flight over "the world of tomorrow." But he wasn't out for a joy ride. There were "a bunch of student gunners on board. And we were supposed to shoot at this sleeve that this other airplane was towing. And I couldn't get the sleeve in my gun sight. So, I told my instructor that. He said, 'Is that what you're going to tell the enemy?'" He laughs. "I said, 'No.'" They gave him a .45 pistol. He took it to the target range. "I couldn't hit anything with it. Probably kill myself."

I didn't know my father in his youth, of course, but I'd have to say that I wouldn't have given him a gun to go to war. He was methodical, careful, a step-by-step guy who understood mechanical things, but he was not a gun guy. He wasn't a pacifist either, but like most city boys, he was not a hunter.

In his last year he told me a surprising story. He had shot a gun before he got to the Air Force, just once. A boy he knew had gotten a BB gun. He let my dad take turns shooting things. Pure boy mischief. His friend had set up some targets—cans and bottles most likely—and shot at them. He hit about half. He gave my father the gun. There was a bird alighting on a fence. Shoot the bird, his friend demanded. He lifted the gun, began to cry, put the gun down and ran home. He didn't want to kill a bird. He came in the house crying. His mother wanted to know what was wrong; he didn't tell her. At his funeral, speaking graveside, I'd thought of mentioning this, but I knew that he wouldn't want it said. This was the last measure of respect I could give, to stand by his generation's rules for what is said and what men take to their graves.

I just made corporal.

## FLYING TO THE ETO

He finished gunnery school and was sent to bomber crew training at Petersen Field in Colorado Springs, Colorado. "What a beautiful country," he said. There's a photo of him there, thin as a reed at nineteen, standing tall in his uniform, beaming. On the back he wrote, "May 1944. I just made corporal here." He probably sent this photo home to his parents.

At Petersen Field the Air Force assembled new bomber crews and trained them in the B-24 for eight weeks before they were sent to fight. Lieutenant Carl E. Vail Jr. led his crew as the pilot. He grew up on the East End of Long Island, New York, in Southold. Vail was an old family name on the East End going back to the 1600s. A Vail had served in almost every American war since the Revolution, when Christopher Vail was captured by the British and imprisoned on a ship in New York Harbor for six months. Vail's father, Carl Vail Sr., was wounded in World War I in a mustard gas attack in France's Argonne Forest a month before the Armistice. That didn't seem to slow him down. In World War II, he served as a lieutenant in the Coast Guard.

His son, Carl Jr., known by his middle name Everett, was crazy about airplanes. He wanted to be a fighter pilot. As part of the Civil Air Patrol he watched the sky for the enemy from the roof of Southold High School. He read anything he could get about flying. Vail had learned to fly the previous year, moving swiftly through the Army Air Forces training, totaling 107 hours in the air. He was a natural born pilot. He'd celebrate his twenty-second birthday while they were training in the B-24.

There were nine other men in the crew. Vail wrote their names in his pilot's logbook: Co-pilot W. E. Barnes; Bombardier S. Mandel; Navigator H. Haney; Engineer V. Treat; Radio Operator H. Lorenz; Nose Gunner R. Kavaras; Waist Gunner P. Mansfield; Ball-turret Gunner N. Miller; Tail gunner, W. Modgling. Crew 4543. They would rely on each other for their lives. Vail knew how to be a leader. He had captained a commercial fishing boat at age sixteen, taking anglers out for the day.

Throughout May and June, they practiced flying in formation with other B-24s—instrument flying, night landings, gunnery, radio navigation, high altitude flying at 18,000 feet, and dropping practice bombs on the bombing range from different altitudes. They flew a practice mission flying a triangular route 144 miles southeast from Denver to La Junta and then sixty-one miles west to Pueblo. Vail's plane was the only one that arrived. Everyone else got lost, including the instructor. Vail would log 230 hours aloft learning to fly the big bomber before they crossed the Atlantic. His training included only thirty-eight hours of instrument flying, which was needed for bad weather.

On July 1 they left for Europe, the ETO, in Army talk, the European Theater of Operations. They left the states a man short. Vail had kicked the bombardier, Mandel, off the crew. He had been hiding during a practice bombing run. The tail gunner had to come forward to do his job. He was trouble; he was out. Mandel, an officer, resisted. Vail had it out with him, telling him that he wasn't worthy of the rest of the crew. They got into a fist fight and Vail beat him up. Vail's superior officers insisted he had to take his bombardier. He refused. The pilot is the captain of the ship. His word is final. They left without Mandel.

They took off and flew over Pike's Peak. "Very turbulent. Everyone threw up," my father recalled. "Can you imagine nine guys throwing up their guts? The pilot had to give the controls to the co-pilot to throw up. I was leaning way out the gunnery window. An officer grabbed my parachute harness and pulled me back—he thought I was jumping. Then he leaned out and threw up. That was about the worst I ever felt," he said.

They flew to Lincoln, Nebraska, and from there on the next day to Manchester, New Hampshire, and Goose Bay, Labrador, before making "the transoceanic flight," as he called it, a phrase right out of the headlines he grew up reading about his aviator heroes.

Over Canada, they were told that they would see the tail of a crashed airplane. "'Don't report it; they know about it.' We saw three tails." They landed in Labrador, in a place that had been left to itself for thousands of years until the war. The "Goose" had been built in a hurry, becoming the busiest airfield in the Western Hemisphere. Thousands of airplanes passed through, flying to England.

They were hungry. The navigator, Lt. Harry Haney, left the plane and bought box lunches for the crew. At age 26, Haney, from Oklahoma, was the "old man" aboard. The plane was refueled, examined, and they were off. "He was sitting at his desk doing his navigating as we flew the ocean.

He doubted himself. We didn't. We had every confidence in him." The Air Force would lose nearly one thousand aircraft over the oceans on the way to battle.

"I'm standing in the middle of the airplane while we were flying, looking out the window. All I could see was ocean. And the tail gunner, we called him Tex, came over to me. He was wearing his parachute harness and carrying his parachute in the other hand: 'We're twenty minutes from land and we don't see anything. So be ready to jump. Just do what I tell you.' At first I thought he was joking." He looked out; still nothing but water. "It looked cold."

He put on his parachute. Tex told him how to jump out of the plane. The Air Force issued parachutes, but there was no training, no practice jumps. "If you have to get out of that plane," one colonel said, "you'll find a hole that a cat couldn't jump through." But wait to open the chute so you're not caught in the slipstream and tangled up in the airplane. After that, remember the Geneva Convention—just give them your name, rank, and serial number. Show them your dog tags. (The Army stamped dog tags with a G.I.'s religion for last rites: P for Protestant, C for Catholic, and H for Hebrew. This left Jews bailing out over Germany with a dilemma. If they tossed their dog tags, they risked being shot as a spy.)

"And all of a sudden, we looked out the window and we saw land. And as we came over the land, on the ground, we could pick out, spelled out with shells and rocks E ... I ... R ... E. That's the Irish Free State. We'd made it."

A little further on they landed at Nutt's Corner, Northern Ireland, nine miles from Belfast. They had been flying twelve hours and ten minutes at an airspeed that was just a third of the average airliner today. "We had just enough fuel to land." They congratulated their navigator. On the ground taxiing, "we followed a jeep that said, *Suivez-moi*, which I knew from my French class meant 'follow me.' We followed the jeep. They pulled us to a parking space." In the bomb bay, there was a gas tank and a big box of K-rations. They each took a box and tucked it into their winter pants and put their feet on Irish ground. July 4, 1944.

"We had this brand-new airplane. We had to sign a 'statement of charges.' If we broke this airplane we had to pay $365,000. We thought this was going to be our airplane. We landed and they took it away. Then we got our airplane, the *Mary Harriet*—Ugly! At the time we all thought it was beautiful." It had already flown dozens of missions, been shot up and patched. It looked a bit lumpish, like some fat, beached sea creature. The Luftwaffe pilots called the B-24 Liberators *dicke autos*, fat cars.

Many bombers had sexy names, saucy names, double entendres, some with "pin-up" paintings of naked and nearly naked women: *Hustlin' Hussy, Heavenly Body, Fertile Myrtle, Hot Stuff, Male Call.* When they got to their assigned airfield, Vail named their plane the *Mary Harriet* for the ground crew chief's girlfriend. He had identified an often-overlooked key to their survival: the mechanics. Vail knew about engines. He'd worked as a mechanic at his father's auto dealership. Once, when the ground crew wanted to replace a blown-out engine with a rebuilt one, he convinced the crew chief to reject it and rebuild their engine himself, a time-consuming job. The *Mary Harriet* would fly sixty-five missions without being recalled for mechanical trouble. The ground crew was awarded a medal for their good work.

The Air Force gave the crew escape kits in case they had to bail out in battle: money, cigarettes, a map, food, prophylactics "in case you got lucky." "You'd better drag it back or don't come back," they lectured them. "Any time the Army did anything for you, they always threatened you with dire consequences." There was also a pistol. "What I was going to do with it, I don't know."

"We spent some time in Ireland practicing our gunfire over the ocean. And admired the young ladies there, whom I noticed didn't wear stockings, but painted their shinbones with rouge. They were beautiful.

"Anyway, nothing about the combat. I flew a few missions until I was injured on one mission and taken off the airplane and put in a hospital. *And that's all the war story you're gonna get from me!*" There my father left it, determined to say no more, except that the past has a way of seeping into the present.

Carl E. Vail Jr.'s crew recently arrived in England.

## FLAME LEAP

My father had arrived in a war-weary kingdom that had endured nightly bombing for ten weeks in the London Blitz and had fought back the prelude to an invasion in the Battle of Britain. The island nation was alone in a Europe that had fallen. He saw blockhouses set up to defend the intersections of small, nameless country roads—nameless because all the street signs had been removed. An English woman he met practiced at the rifle range each Wednesday night. These were the first signs he saw of the war.

Along the way the Army had given the men a slim booklet, *A Short Guide to Great Britain*, written, in part, by the English author of *Lassie Come Home*, Eric Knight. The guide says right off that if you're Irish American, forget "old grievances." "There is no time today to fight old wars over again." It steps quickly through history—"Our ideals of religious freedom were all brought from Britain when the Pilgrims landed at Plymouth Rock . . . and parts of our own Bill of Rights were borrowed from the great charters of British liberty." It gives some language pointers—"It isn't a good idea . . . to say 'bloody' in mixed company in Britain—it is one of their worst swear words." And it repeatedly cautions Yanks about being rude:

> *You are coming to Britain from a country where your home is still safe, food is still plentiful, and lights are still burning. So, it is doubly important for you to remember that the British soldiers and civilians have been living under a tremendous strain. It is always impolite to criticize your hosts. It is militarily stupid to insult your allies. So, stop and think before you sound off about lukewarm beer, or cold boiled potatoes, or the way English cigarettes taste.*

Put away your comments about dreary British weather, dinky cars, worn-out trains, shabby dress, confusing currency, and bland food: "The British don't know how to make a good cup of coffee. You don't know how to make a good cup of tea. It's an even swap." And "keep out of arguments. . . . Never criticize the King or the Queen."

Above all, don't be a show-off:

> *You are higher paid than the British 'Tommy.' Don't rub it in. . . . Don't show off or brag or bluster—'swank' as the British say. If somebody looks in your direction and says, 'He's chucking his weight about,' you can be pretty sure you're off base. That's the time to pull in your ears.*
>
> *The British will welcome you as friends and allies. But remember that crossing the ocean doesn't automatically make you a hero. There are housewives in aprons and youngsters in knee pants . . . who have lived through more high explosives in air raids than many soldiers saw in first class barrages in the last war.*
>
> *Remember there's a war on. Britain may look a little shop-worn and grimy to you. The British people are anxious to have you know that you are not seeing its country at its best. There's been a war on since 1939. The houses haven't been painted because factories are not making paint—they're making planes. The famous English gardens and parks are either unkept because there are no men to take care of*

*them, or they are being used to grow needed vegetables. . . . In normal times Britain looks much prettier, cleaner, neater.*

They were sent to join the 453rd BG at the U.S. Army Air Station at Old Buckenham (pronounced: *buck-un-um).* "Old Buc" was one of a hundred airfields for bombers and fighters newly built in East Anglia, an isolated region of low-lying farms, watery fens, and windmills that shared a kinship with Holland across the North Sea. East Anglia was only a hundred miles or so from London, but to the Brits it was a backwater of stubborn farmers, a place where horse-drawn plows were more common than tractors.

The airfields were built fast, almost nonstop, by construction crews working in two, ten-hour shifts starting before first light, pausing for meals brought to them in the field, in haste to destroy an ancient land-scape of farms and cottages, forests and hedgerows. At the peak, a new airfield was begun every three days. Some farmers resisted, holding off the first surveyors with shotguns, but they relented. They had no choice; there was a war on. Building the airfields was "the biggest civil works program in the history of Great Britain," says one historian.

By D-Day, there was an airfield every eight miles, on average, in East Anglia. The villagers by the bases found themselves outnumbered by Americans by as much as one hundred to one. In 1944, one in seven residents of the East Anglia county of Suffolk was a Yank. In Bomber County, as some residents called it, every old road seemed to lead to an airfield. Three million U.S. servicemen would pass through Britain.

Old Buc was laid out in a standard configuration, with three concrete runways: the main 6,000-foot runway, fifty yards wide, headed southwest to northeast, and two auxiliary runways 5,200 feet each, completing a triangle. This was encircled by a concrete taxiway. Fifty "hardstands" for B-24s were dispersed in small groups alongside this perimeter track in case of attack. (The Luftwaffe hit the airfield in March 1944 and repeatedly bombed the nearby city of Norwich. There were also trenches for men to take cover.) There was a two-story control tower—call sign Flame Leap—and metal Quonset huts and their British counterpart (Nissen huts), prefabricated concrete Maycrete buildings, two large metal hangars, headquarters, mess, briefing halls, parachute and equipment stores, engineering and carpenters' workshops, bomb and turret trainers, a hospital, officers and enlisted men's clubs, post exchange (PX), chapel, movie theatre, and a gym. Nearly three thousand men were assigned to Old Buc; more than half were the ground support. Just a year before, this land had been Abbey Farm, Woodhall Farm, and Island House—all demolished, along with the hedgerows and the trees.

Shadowing the taxiway for a short stretch was Bunn's Bank, a slight ridge just a few feet high and twenty feet wide. Bunn's Bank, like the airfield, was a military structure of its era. It was believed to have been built in the ninth century by King Edmund, the last king of the East Angles, to defend against the Vikings. Few of the new occupants noticed it, but the windmill by Carleton Rode was a ready-made flier's landmark.

The first men arriving at the newly opened, but unfinished, airfield in December 1943 had left the sunshine and plenty of Southern California to endure a winter of endless rain, "penetrating cold," and mud. The men "trudged through ankle deep to knee deep mud a good part of the time." If they didn't have a bike, they had to walk over a mile to their airplane, and a "good half mile to the mess hall and too often cold showers." Further adding to the "demoralized atmosphere, it was two days before Christmas." The main muddy lane was known as Overshoe Lane (and sometimes Hipboot Lane). It met Miller Road at a big puddle, an intersection called Old Swimming Hole. Colds and flu were rampant. The men could see their breath in the sleeping huts.

The men slept twelve to a hut, enlisted and officers in separate huts, usually in narrow cots with biscuit-thin canvas mattresses. Everyone relied on the same small coal stoves to push back the damp chill. Coal was rationed, and at some airfields forbidden because it was needed to run munitions factories, leaving coke (harder to light and keep going) at Old Buc for the "tortoises" as the British called the stoves. To stay warm, a week's ration of coal or coke could be burned in just one night. A Nissen hut was like "an icebox open at both ends."

Each hut had a couple of folding tables and a radio. The men listened to ARN, the American Radio Network, out of London or the BBC's "unswingy swing." The best blues, swing, and Dixieland was on the

German stations. Mascot pets were common—puppies, parrots, rabbits, skunks, monkeys, and ferrets. Their owners changed frequently as men didn't return. Old Buc's lucky mascot was a puppy named Spare Parts, a small black or brown spaniel-like dog with white paws.

The huts were decorated with pin-up girls and black-and-white photos of girlfriends and wives. Over a bunk might be the common-enough sight of marks counting down the missions made by an airman no longer with them—"gone down" is what they'd say. They wouldn't say "killed." "It's strange to sleep in the bunk of a man who was at breakfast with you and is now dead or a prisoner hundreds of miles away," reported John Steinbeck. "It's strange but necessary." (One new crew came in and didn't even get to unpack. They were lost on their first mission before anyone could learn their names.)

There was a lot of waiting around in the Bomber War, waiting out the foggy soup of rainy days, which cut flying days almost in half. They slept in on bad weather days, played poker and blackjack, tried to iron their shirts, and wrote letters, which were read by a censor. They lay in their "sacks" talking of home and how many missions they "had in" and how many "to go." And they talked about flak and fighters. ("Who's afraid of the new Focke-Wulf?"—the German fighter plane—asked a poster aimed at morale boosting, to which one wag had attached a sheet: "Sign here.")

"Sacks contribute, certainly, their share to the odor which universally permeates the Nissen huts of combat crews," wrote Sergeants Bud Hutton and Andy Rooney. "So do the bundles of laundry behind the bunks, always going to the wash next week. So do the leather flying clothes, the dampness of the land, the burning combination of coke and/or coal and/or wood, the thickly eddying wall of tobacco smoke, the hair oil the inevitable dude uses, and possibly most of all the acid-sharp odor that arises from bodies whose owners more often than not feel fear within them. . . . It is not a bad smell." It was the smell of home. "You always, as long as you can, go back to it."

The Air Force closely monitored the morale of its airmen. A drop in morale, however that was measured, was taken seriously by the commanding officers. They received a running narrative of activities at the airfields, upbeat reports written sometimes like a jaunty yearbook or like one of the gossip columnists of the era. Everyone is having a swell time at Old Buc, at the movies, the library "with its many volumes of good literature," USO shows, glee club, an art show (with more than sixty entries), dances, lectures, Sunday evening "classical radio sessions," bridge club, bingo, softball, tennis and ping-pong tourneys. (Overcoming a shortage of ping-pong balls, Old Buc's team won the title in the 2nd Air Division.)

A September 1944 report from Old Buc boasts that "even ice cream was served occasionally. Sunday chicken dinner was now a habit. The road had dried enough to permit paving. That promised to do away completely with mud." The Aero Club gave two dances. "The base band, The G.I.'Vers—a pun on 'jive'—played while the G.I.s danced. Their partners included Wrens [Women's Royal Naval Service] from Great Yarmouth, as well as girls from nearby Attleborough, Wymondham, Norwich, and Old Buckenham. Everyone agreed that the dances were improving." At the NCO (Non-Commissioned Officers') Club, "Miss Katherine Dionne . . . started the fad of free waffles once weekly. Needless to say, the men ate it up. In three weeks, they consumed 1,700 waffles." The Officers' Club was "well stocked with Scotch, Rye and beer." And Tuesday night lectures included a report from a lieutenant just back from the states. "His caricatures of the folks back home and comic descriptions of their 'struggle to live' brought many a burst of laughter from his audience."

The Air Force sounds like a sleep-away summer camp in these dispatches, but one with a high mortality rate. A member of the 15th Air Force, based in Southern Italy, presented one day of war at their field, March 3, 1944. As they left for a mission, one of their bombers, "apparently unable to get up off the runway . . . burst into a sheet of flame, keeled over on its nose, and exploded. It was total destruction and death in a matter of seconds. We lost one of our most capable and best-liked pilots, Lt. Jimmy Isbell, short, wiry and Irish-faced—and his entire crew." This was the seventh crew that they had lost. They had only started flying two months earlier in January. Only ten of their original crews remained.

That evening, after "special services," "the boys" were entertained by a USO show. "The main attraction (female) went through the chow line for supper and"—as reported in the language of the era—"morale took a sudden zoom at the appearance of a real American chassis."

Mostly, the airmen missed a lot of these activities. They didn't go to the Red Cross club for bingo run by the Red Cross "girls" who tried "to be a sort of remote combination of Rita Hayworth and your best friend's big sister," said Hutton and Rooney. Most didn't get out of their sacks. They were just too tired after flying a mission. They were so tired that Hutton and Rooney figured that less than half wanted to "chase girls." "A good number" spent leave time in English homes.

I'm guessing that my father never went to any lectures, though he may have looked over the art show. I just can't imagine that when Lord Ironside arrived to talk about India that this retired British Army commander drew a crowd among the enlisted men. If I was spending what might be my last night on earth—a thought that some of the airmen carried with them—I wouldn't spend it listening to Lord Ironside, even if he had a grand name.

And this was part of the oddity of the Air War, the commute to battle. The infantry in the field wasn't being entertained, except by the occasional USO tour. The chirpy dispatches about waffle breakfasts, dances, and journeys to the pub, and calling Old Buc "home" stand in for what can't be said: this was an unprecedented way of war and it was difficult to know if it was succeeding, if it was worth their lives.

There are occasional revealing references in the dispatches, like to a navigator "who thought too much about the war." So, there was a right way to think about the war, which was not too much, which was to leave the day's carnage behind you, just get some sleep, go get a drink at the officers' club, and start all over again. *Don't think about it.* That's what Fred Rochlin, a B-24 navigator, was told. "First, you follow orders and do what you've been trained to do. Then just forget it. Forget it. And if you can't, then pretend."

The Air Force, even if it was part of the Army, was separate, going light on many of the Army's formalities. What mattered was what happened in the air—strict attention to flying in tight formations, arriving over the target, and bombing accurately. On the ground, the airmen didn't think of themselves as soldiers. At a dance, my father went in, holding out his hand, offering a dance to some women waiting on a bench. "The young lady came to me and said, 'Hi soldier.' Because I was an airman, I wasn't used to being called a soldier."

The airfields may have been chilly, damp, and sometimes muddy, but for a wartime posting, this was comfortable. "The boys were warm, clean, well fed; their life was dangerous and not very romantic to them, and between missions they got homesick and sometimes bored," reported Ernie Pyle. "But even so they had a pretty good time with their live young spirits, and they were grateful that they could live as well and have as much pleasure as they did have. For they knew that anything good in wartime is just that much velvet.

"A man approached death rather decently in the Air Forces. He died well-fed and clean-shaven, if that was any comfort," wrote Pyle. "He was at the front only a few hours of the day, instead of day and night for months on end. . . . But in the infantry a soldier had to become half beast in order to survive."

At Old Buc my father took up residence at the intersection of routine and sudden death. He flew "home" to land where, close to the runway, the farmers were busy haying as they had done for centuries. Which was the true routine? He returned to a field that had a companion fortification, Bunn's Bank from the ninth century, King Edmund's stand against the Vikings. He was playing his part in centuries of warfare. War was a routine, too.

After arriving at Old Buc, Vail and his crew practiced formation flying for the next few weeks. They flew their first mission a month after landing in Northern Ireland, but they were still learning. After their first four missions, they were back to flying practice formations.

In the months before they had arrived, the 453rd was having problems. On March 18, the Group Commander, Col. Joseph A. Miller, leading a mission to bomb Friedrichshafen, Germany, crashed his shot-up bomber in France and was captured. Miller had led the 453rd from its start. Second Division headquarters chose a new leader, making an unusual choice by promoting a young pilot with combat experience over an older commissioned officer who had started in a military academy. Lieutenant Col. Ramsay A. Potts had seen serious combat and was one of the Air Force's most decorated officers. Potts was a flight leader in the daring raid on the Ploesti oil refineries in Romania.

Ploesti was heavily defended with more anti-aircraft flak guns than Berlin, something the intelligence reports had missed. This was early in the war for the Air Force and the bombers were still flying without any fighter support. One hundred seventy-eight B-24s took off from Northern Africa on August 1, 1943, flying low under the radar. Fifty-four planes never returned. Of the 1,726 men on the mission, 310 were killed, 130 wounded, and 186 were prisoners of war. Ploesti was seriously damaged but the Nazis, using ten thousand slaves, rebuilt it within weeks. Since that mission, Potts, at age twenty-seven, had flown a full combat tour, but he was reluctant to take command of the 453rd. All the other group commanders, like his predecessor Miller, were West Pointers, and they were older. One officer at division headquarters doubted that he'd last more than six weeks.

He found a troubled unit. The 453rd was "not flying very well together as a group," said Potts. "They had a considerable number of individually skilled pilots and crews, and also they had pretty good maintenance, but they had very poor organization." And they had a morale problem. Seven officers refused to fly any more, and it was rumored that another dozen were thinking of joining them. Potts spoke to the men and got all but one back into the air. Next, he removed the entire 453rd from combat.

"I got permission from the division commander to stand down from flying combat missions and immediately started flying training missions, which was very irksome to the people in the group there, but we ironed out some problems and troubles." In an attempt to bring order to Old Buc, Potts removed all the bicycles—except his. The men responded by scooping up his bike and, during a practice mission, dropping it into the English Channel.

Potts was undeterred. "We got the group finally whipped into shape, and began a series of very intensive operations," he said.

*We didn't have a morale problem after a little while. . . . This was the period just before D-Day, and we were flying against German airfields, we were flying against the V-1 and V-2 sites, we were flying against some oil targets, we were flying against marshaling and transportation targets in preparation for invasion. . . . I was flying occasional missions myself, but I was mainly engaged in a tremendous effort to organize the group and give them a feeling of confidence in themselves and really develop the cohesion needed to function as a unit. We did this. I honestly don't believe I got more than five hours of sleep per night during that whole period of three and a half months there.*

Potts made the "453rd a winner," said Starr Smith, who served under Potts as an intelligence officer preparing the mission briefings. Potts and his assisting officer "were on the job around the clock, constantly on the move, often . . . on the flight line, checking every detail, laying on practice missions—seldom leaving the base. Everybody worked. Everybody was overworked. Changes came. Morale was high. Spirits soared. Target proficiency improved." Another officer said, "the change at Old Buc after Ramsay . . . came in was like daylight and dark."

He succeeded, but it took its toll. He was exhausted. "They sent me home on what was known as 'thirty days rest and recreation.' . . . I guess I stayed about ten days and didn't get any rest or any real recreation. I was still all keyed up and felt like I ought to get back to the scene of action." He returned to England and took command of another group.

Potts left the 453rd with an important lesson, one taken from

*Marshal Montgomery's view of war. Monty used to go up to a soldier and ask him what was the most important thing he had? And when the soldier would invariably answer something like his rifle, Monty would jump all over him and say, no it wasn't, it was your life, so you*

*better hold on to it. I told the 453rd the same thing until it was coming out of their ears. From a military point of view, that meant they better fly in close formation if they expected to return to base.*

They needed to win the war and to do that they had to stay alive. That was his message "and more than that an officer can't do."

My father knew none of this. He was a teenager, away from home for the first time, learning to be an air gunner. His father Elai, who was a milliner, a hat maker in an era of lavish women's hats, wanted to help his only son, so he offered to sew garrison caps for the crew of the *Mary Harriet*. My father gathered up their hat sizes and wrote back with the sizes for six caps. His father wrote back to him: "What's wrong with you? Aren't there ten men on your airplane?" "Well, four are officers," my father replied—officers wore billed caps. His father lit into him: "You're flying with those men." This was only one of two times in his life that his father had scolded him, he said. (The other was for missing a vote.)

Elai and Ida also sent a box of scarce items to a family near Old Buc who had taken to looking after their son. Quite a few English families near the airfields took care of "the boys," sharing their homes and meals when everything was in short supply. "So, they sent what I call a care package," he said, "Lux soap, nylon stockings, tobacco, some chocolate, a couple of other things. And they were very grateful for that." They had also sent tea in bags. This was received warily: Tea in a paper bag? To put in the water? Was that "sanitary?"

Forty years later, when I was going to England to visit some friends there, he asked, "Do they need anything?" He knew otherwise, of course, but the memories of wartime England were indelible. England in 1944, on rationing, under the bombs, lived somewhere within him. He never went back.

# 2

# THE AIR WAR

## SCHWERIN AND BRUNSWICK

HE FLEW HIS FIRST MISSION ON AUGUST 4, 1944, ONE MONTH AFTER HE had arrived in Ireland, and eight months since he had enlisted. He was at his position as a "L.W.G.," a left waist gunner. In the handwritten dairy I had found in his dresser drawer, he wrote:

Mission number 1.

The *Mary Harriet*, carrying ten 500-pound bombs, joined eighty-eight other bombers attacking a factory assembling Focke-Wulf 190s in Schwerin, Germany, on a day that was "C.A.V.U."—Ceiling and Visibility Unlimited (after they took off in fog). The Fw 190, called by its pilots the Wurger—Shrike (the "Butcher Bird")—was one of the best, most effective fighters in the war, feared by the Allies. "The target was left practically entirely enveloped in smoke," said the first intelligence report. "Very good results." The aircraft factory was just one of more than twenty targets that day, including other aircraft and torpedo factories, oil refineries, a bridge, railroad yards, batteries of guns on the coast, and V-1 and V-2 missile sites, which were attacked by more than 1,100 bombers and 746 fighters.

The fighters were in "big air battles" with "dogfights all over the sky," chasing the Messerschmitt Me 109s away from the bombers and following them "right down to the deck," where they twisted around in "tight circles" until they recorded a kill, said the Eighth Air Force press release, which quoted the fighter pilots' lively stories and noted their hometowns, so the news would reach the folks back in Clint, Texas, and Cape Elizabeth, Maine. The Air Force sent out "hometown stories" by the thousands—five thousand in August 1944 alone, including "labor-morale" stories to motivate the factory workers building B-24 Liberators.

Fifteen bombers and fifteen fighters were lost, and about a third of the bombers, more than four hundred, flew home riddled with holes from the anti-aircraft guns. Eight airmen were dead, twelve wounded, and 148 were missing in action (MIA). The *Mary Harriet* was in the air for seven hours and twenty-five minutes without incident, except for nearly colliding with another bomber in the air, which my father called *Carley*. (The 453rd had no planes by that name; it was likely *Curly*.) "This scared me more than all the flak I saw," he wrote. "Extremely cold in the waist," the large gun port that was about the size of a picture window and open to the weather four miles up.

In three weeks, on August 25, *Curly* would narrowly escape being shot down when it was hit by flak over the Zuider Zee. "The number four engine failed immediately," said pilot Eino Alve. "The bomb doors were partly torn loose and began to flap wildly. A fuel line was severed and the bomb bay was filled with gasoline and vapors. . . . We could explode any minute. . . . The flapping of the bomb doors could cause a spark and that would be the end of all of us." Two crewmen saved the ship. Engineer Bill Heerts gripped radio operator Bob Jordan by his parachute harness as he "hung out over space to kick the doors free."

*Curly* left the formation. They jettisoned their bombs in a heavily wooded area and were left flying alone, "an easy target" for the Luftwaffe.

> *[A] fighter plane did pick us up, but thank God it was American not German. He was flying a P-47 and came within eyeball range. He called over the radio, "Hello big friend, this is your little friend. How much fuel do you have?" Just then a flak battery had our range again and began firing—hoping to finish us off. Our "little friend" dove earthward, heading directly toward our enemy. His courage and skill put a stop to the German firing. We were saved.*

On two engines, Alve and his copilot held the B-24 level at 10,000 feet. "In the distance I could see a sight that never looked better to these weary eyes—the White Cliffs of Dover. We were home!"

They made it back to Old Buckenham, where they landed with no brakes or flaps. The crew thought the plane was a total loss, but *Curly* was flying again in two weeks.

The *Mary Harriet* was hit by flak the next day. "Four flak holes. One in rite [sic] vertical stabilizer, 2 near camera hatch, one in nose," my father noted. "Heard flak explode. Scared at first, later mad as a whet [sic] hen." They were bombing the Daimler-Benz aircraft engine plant in Brunswick, part of a larger force of more than 1,100 bombers, and 646 fighters attacking the region's oil refineries and aircraft and tank factories. "Results—Numerous fires started. Good," he wrote. More than forty percent of the bombers were shot up by flak guns or attacking fighters. Thirteen bombers and four fighters went down. Eighteen men were reported as killed, 109 MIA, and nineteen were wounded.

## FROM THE BOOK OF CHANCE

The German anti-aircraft guns had a hold on the Eighth Air Force. The Eighth issued flak reports that sounded like weather forecasts. Here's the flak report for September 10, 1944, when my father flew to Ulm in southwest Germany:

Ulm—meager, fairly accurate.

Heilbronn—meager, fairly accurate.

Furth—meager to moderate, inaccurate.

Sindelfingen—moderate to intense, accurate.

And so on through another eighteen cities and towns with reported flak varying from light to heavy, meager to moderate to intense, inaccurate to accurate.

The reported intensity and accuracy of flak varied from man to man in the same crew. There were no standards. How do you measure flak? In some ways the reports may have been a psychological portrait—*whoa* that was close. When one shell burst right under his plane, a navigator reported, "I thought someone hit me with a baseball bat. The concussion was so terrific." And a waist gunner, riding through another attack, said, "At 40 degrees below zero, you can sweat."

Flak hit the big bombers in a rain of steel pellets. It sounded like hail on a tin roof, like BBs rolling around, said the airmen. It could tear into the bomber's aluminum skin with a "shriek" or a "hissing." It could splatter the head of your pilot or miss by an inch. Loose, hot steel rattling around, as if your anxieties had taken shape. It was lethal with a randomness that was cruel. They could smell the flak through their oxygen masks.

The German anti-aircraft gunners filled the sky with explosions and steel. Nearly a million men and women were committed to the guns. In the last years of the war, the 88mm guns were grouped in *Grossbatterien* of twelve, sixteen, eighteen, or twenty-four—a huge shotgun firing thousands of rounds—tons of explosives a minute—four or five miles high. Major targets were surrounded by two hundred guns; oil refineries by 450 guns, and so many guns guarded the factories in the Ruhr Valley that it was known as Flak Alley. The guns had an effect; the Air Force found that flak reduced bombing accuracy by 10 to 20 percent. The big guns rattled the fliers; they were missing their targets.

Each exploding shell launched about 1,500 metal fragments. Some would pass right through the plane, or explode inside, and some shells brought a rain of fire. If they were close enough to see the red center of the dark cloud, they expected to be hit. This could be what hell looks like, thought Lt. Col. George McGovern, a B-24 pilot who flew thirty-five missions and was awarded the Distinguished Flying Cross. "Hell can't be any worse than that." An unnamed crewman, in another battle, was more direct when he said over the plane's intercom, "Mary, Mother of God, get me out of this."

The bombers sometimes returned with hundreds of holes, with engines out or on fire, with ruptured fuel lines and cut rudder cables, with men wounded, maimed, and bleeding to death. On "good missions" with "meager flak" and few of the Luftwaffe's fighters attacking, bombers and fighters could still be lost or "missing in action." Seven bombers and four fighters on one mission, nine bombers and three fighters on another "good mission," as many as ninety-three men "missing." Telegrams sent to Ada, Oklahoma; Palo Alto, California; Grand Rapids, Michigan; Hillsboro, Texas: "We regret to inform you. . . ."

On average, one quarter of the Eighth Air Force's bombers were hit by flak. The B-24, which couldn't fly as high as the B-17, was more vulnerable. Most were patched and sent back out; late in the war one in thirteen was destroyed. In August 1944, when my father began flying in combat, flak damage peaked. The Eighth Air Force lost 316 bombers, more than three thousand men, to flak that August.

Flak inflicted close to three-quarters of all the wounds in the Eighth Air Force. Your fate depended on where you were in the bomber. Each waist gunner, standing at the open windows, had about a 10 percent chance of being hit. Bombardiers took 15 percent of the hits, followed by the navigator (13.2 percent), rear gunner (12.6 percent), the top gunner (8.3 percent), pilot (7.7 percent), copilot (6.2 percent), and the least likely to be hit, the low-hanging ball turret gunner (5.5 percent). They were most often hit in the legs (44 percent of all wounds). Twenty percent would die of those wounds. Close to a third would be hit in the arms with about a third dying. Chest injuries (21 percent) had a lower fatality rate (9 percent), due to protection from flak vests.

Until June 1944 fighters destroyed and damaged more bombers than flak, the statistics said, but the statistics were compiled on the ground and couldn't account for the gut-tightening fear as your crew flew a straight and level approach to the target through the dark cloud bursts. They just had to sit there and take it and fly through. "We could not hide," said nose gunner Lt. Thomas Neilan. "We were simply marooned aloft in an aluminum coffin that seemed to creep as slowly across the sky as a fly across the wall; vulnerable to all who wanted to shoot us down." Gunners could shoot at fighters, but flak reduced them to helpless spectators. Frustrated, they'd open fire at puffs of smoke. Neilan watched the fireball bursts and black smoke rolling, reaching out to his plane. "I would find myself saying, 'the next one is it. Can't miss next time. This is it.'" Flak was a terror.

The flak-filled skies followed the bomber crews back to England. When the airmen were flak happy (shaken up), they were sent to flak homes or flak farms on flak leave for a week's "R & R" (rest and relaxation). At briefings they studied the Flak Zone over a target, looking at the Flak Maps. They carried the word into battle flying B-17s named: *Flack Alley, Flack Alley II, Flak Alley Lil'* (2 of those), *Flak Alley Lil' II, Flack Buster, Flak Dancer* (2), *Flak Dodger* (4), *Flak Eater, Flak Evader, Flak Fed Gal, Flak Flirter, Flak Fobic, Flak Hack* (2), *Flak Happy* (8), *Flak Happy II, Flak Happy Pappy, Flak Heaven, Flak Hopper* (2), *Flak House* (2), *Flak Magic, Flak Magnet* (2), *Flak Magnet II, Flak No. 2, Flak Off Limits, Flak Palace, Flak Plow, Flak Queen, Flak Rabbit, Flak Rat, Flak Rat II, Flack Sack, Flak Sak, Flack Shack* (2), *Flak Shack* (3), *Flak Shy, Flak Shy Lady, Flak Suit, Flak-Wolf, Flakstop, Mac's Flak Shak, Miss Flak, Old Flak Magnet, Ole Flak Sack, Ole Scatter Flak*, and so on.

They parodied their fears by singing tunes like "As Flak Goes By":

> You must remember this
> The flak can't always miss
> Somebody's gotta' die.

And they carried their fears into their sleep. They had "flak dreams," said Hutton and Rooney in a wartime book. "You doze off in your sack and pretty soon the F-Ws begin to bore in at you, cannon flashing, and the flak begins to come up in close black puffs; or maybe you find yourself endlessly falling through space, tearing at a parachute which never opens."

The stories of flak are a literature of near misses, of geometry, chance, and luck. It was a universe in which an inch or two separated life and death or injury.

The Eighth Air Force fed quotes to the press from the pilots and crews of the bombers. The quotes usually said: *Flak was everywhere, but it missed us. Flak was so thick you could walk on it; the sky was black with flak; we were shot up, but we made it back. Flak grazed my face, my leg, sliced my sleeve and glove to ribbons, but I'm OK. It ripped off my oxygen mask, just missing my Adam's apple. I can't figure out how it missed me. It tore a hole in the map I was reading but didn't touch me. I bent down to pull up a sock and flak smashed the windows where my head had been. I'd be dead if I hadn't ducked.*

Kurt Wolf was a tail gunner on a B-17. He was part of the 452nd Bomber Group based just seven miles from the 453rd at Old Buckenham. Wool socks saved his life. He had gotten a pair sent from home. Wool socks were scarce. He was sitting at his gun in the small glass canopy on the tail of the plane when he felt that his right sock had fallen. It had "crawled down in my boot," he said. At thirty-five below zero, this could be serious. "I leaned down to pull that sock back up and just as I leaned down . . . a piece of shrapnel took out both those windows where my head was. So that pair of socks saved my life." That's how he told the story when he was eighty-seven years old.

The flak stories are like that tale of a fallen sock. The flak was heavy, was accurate, was moderate, light, inaccurate, was everywhere. There was no empty air. The sky was a maze of thick flak smoke. But I'm alive—that was the unstated refrain. And unspoken—for now.

Chance, fate, luck, and near misses live in the vets' stories—the pilot assigned to the squadron's "coffin corner" of the formation whose position is switched at the last moment and is saved, the shards of flak twisting through the airplane cockpit missing by an inch or less, the navigator pulled from the English Channel by an RAF rescue launch seconds before he drowned.

Minutes. Inches. Banal changes that meant life or death. Back in the peacetime world—working nine-to-five, taking children to get shoes—how could the veterans explain that they were only in this life by a few inches? It was as though they'd realized, years before the physicists' theories, that many universes exist side by side—the world with them and the world without them. They saw it and they had no words for it.

## FREVENT AND STRASBOURG

On his next two missions they were defeated by cloud cover. They could not drop their bombs. They flew to railroad marshalling yards in Frevent, France, on August 7, and to Strasbourg on the ninth. Over Frevent, only twelve of the thirty-six bombers dispatched by the 453rd found enough of a break in the clouds to see the rail yard. The *Mary Harriet* returned with its full load of eight 1,000-pound bombs. The flak from four-gun batteries was "extremely accurate," my father wrote. "Scared as usual" and cold. "Was sorry I wasn't wearing flak suit."

On the ninth, they were recalled before they reached Strasbourg. "Whole mission snafued by bad ship," he wrote, without elaborating. "Had a notion to shoot at 2 P-38s," their supporting fighters. When the 453rd broke out of the clouds, said Capt. Richard Bickerstaff, who was leading, "my formation was all over the sky and by the time we got together again we were far in trail of the lead group" with worse weather ahead, so they returned. The mission was recalled, but if they had entered enemy territory it would count, bringing them closer to going home.

## THE COMBAT BOX

Each mission began with the "damage book," the reconnaissance photos and the analysis of what had been bombed and what needed to be bombed again. The bombers would hit a factory or a railroad marshalling yard with varying degrees of effectiveness. The Nazis would rebuild or reorganize their industry and the cycle would repeat. For example, it could take five or six raids to destroy a railroad yard. The commanding general and his staff studied the "damage book" and the Supreme Allied Command's priorities.

Sending out hundreds of bombers and fighters took days of planning, and sometimes months of debate. The Eighth Air Force's planners worked in an underground war room at the headquarters in High Wycombe, a grand country house outside London (code name "Pinetree"). Their decisions would direct nearly two-hundred-thousand men, and ultimately when the war would be won. The Air Force was a corporation that had to plan its production daily.

The mission orders were passed down through the chain of command from the Chief of Operations. He made the final decision early in the evening before the next day's planned raid. Weather was a tricky call. It rained an average of fourteen days a month. They wanted to have clear skies over England in the morning to take-off and late to return, and semi-cloudy, at least, over the target. (As airborne radar was adopted in late 1943, more missions were flown on overcast days.) The forecast would be reviewed again late at night.

An advance warning went out, in code, on the teleprinter to the three air divisions. They then alerted the combat wings, which then alerted the individual bomb groups. At each level, the mission took shape. The air divisions determined the number of bombers needed and the type and tonnage of the bombs. They also coordinated the fighter support. Working through the night behind blackout curtains, the bomb group's officers chose the crews and their place in the formation, calculated the assembly times and mapped the route. The official, more detailed, field order followed sometimes as much as seven or eight hours later with a yard or more of yellow paper spilling out of the teleprinter.

While they were planning the mission, the ordnance, armament, and maintenance crews were working through the night, from eleven until four or five in the morning, loading the five-hundred or thousand-pound bombs, the long belts of machine gun ammunition, patching flak holes, fueling the plane, and testing the engines.

The airmen would be woken up at 3:00 a.m. for breakfast—fresh eggs on mission mornings, "combat eggs," instead of powdered "square eggs."

Some men didn't eat a thing, and others ate like it was their last meal. "You could hear a pin drop," a crewman remembered. "You had a 50 percent chance of returning. You don't want to think about it, but it's there." My father recalled one morning like this:

*They woke us at 3:30 in the morning and told us to get on down to the mess hall. A Maximum Effort has been called. That means any airplane that could fly was going to be in the air. So we all got on our bicycles and went over to the mess hall and got on line. And when I got to my turn to tell the cook what I wanted, he said to me, "How do you want your eggs? Scrambled or over easy or what?" The guy behind me says, "I think we're getting killed today because they never ask us how we want our eggs." I thought that was funny, at the time anyway.*

*On our way over to the mess hall we saw Royal Air Force bombers returning from missions. They returned and flew over our base. The Royal Air Force bombed the enemy at night. We bombed them during the day. How effective this all was has been written about by many people and nobody really knows. I just know it killed a lot of people.*

After breakfast, the flight crew officers filed into the briefing room to wait for the group commander. They sat sweating in heavy suits and boots, smelling of shaving lotion and hair oil. The air was thick with cigarette smoke.

The commander, a full colonel, entered as the men stood at attention and then sat down. After an officer pulled the curtain open in front of a map revealing the target and route, the commander described their mission. An intelligence officer then reviewed the target in detail. The locations of the anti-aircraft guns were pointed out on the map. Fighter support and possible enemy aircraft were noted. The weather officer followed, giving them the winds and visibility on the route and at the target. The men were told who the lead pilot would be and then they synchronized their watches when an officer called out "hack!" Some men met with their chaplains for a prayer and a blessing. They went to the equipment sheds to get escape kits, oxygen masks, electric suits, flak jackets, helmets, and parachutes. They turned in their valuables and their identification cards. They might leave a letter behind with a friend for their family. The pilot briefed the enlisted men in his crew at the plane.

The pilot and copilot started the four engines about twenty-five minutes before they took off, running through the checklist. This was a "two-man job," said B-24 pilot Lt. Col. William E. Carigan Jr. "Both pilots are busy with both hands; the copilot with all the mechanical things—sequences of fuel boosters, primers, energizing and meshing starters; the pilot with mixtures and throttles, which require some touch." After that, the B-24 required "considerable muscle," said Carigan. It called for "more muscle to fly than does any other airplane." It was "sternly unforgiving and demanding."

As they taxied, the bomb bay doors were open to vent fumes. The lead squadron went first. The control tower fired a flare and the big bombers—thirty-five tons at their maximum "war emergency" weight—began moving down the runway toward take-off speed—160 mph—just seconds apart, closer than at any airport today. "What sounded like a charging bull was actually more akin to a duck beginning to waddle. It was agonizingly slow," said pilot Eino Alve.

*So, you hunched and rocked back and forth in your seat, in a futile attempt to nudge the plane forward faster. Standing behind you and to your right, the engineer watched the engines' health on the instruments. The co-pilot watched the airspeed indicator, calling out its advancing numbers: 70, 80, 90 . . . and then you were committed. Even if you lost an engine, you'd have no choice but to try to take off.*

Every nut and bolt rattled as they climbed toward the assigned altitude and flew an ascending spiral following a radio beacon as they found their position. They might have to circle this radio beacon, called a "buncher," several times waiting for all the bombers to assemble.

The key to the Air Force's campaign was the formation, eighteen or more bombers flying about a dozen yards apart to form a box, like a fort with many guns, aimed in every direction. It was supposed to be impenetrable, like a fortress guarding a harbor. Formation flying also concentrated the bombs on the target. Each formation would join other formations, each with its own time to arrive at the target. The shape of the "combat box" and the number of planes changed throughout the war. Bombardment division and wing leaders were allowed to experiment. Staying in formation was essential. On some missions, half of the bombers that were shot down were stragglers, lone antelopes, separated from the herd, vulnerable to the lions.

"Apparently the weakest aspect of our recent operations has been the extremely poor formation flying," said a critique by the Group Commanders of the 389th, 445th, and 453rd in June 1944. "This is an evil which runs in cycles and evidence clearly indicates that we must begin another strenuous campaign to improve. . . . The quality of formation flying is of greatest importance to the success of any operational mission in every way, beginning with the precision of bombing and the degree of security attained." Vail's pilot logbook shows him flying frequent formation practice between combat missions.

Getting hundreds of airplanes into the right order in the sky could take an hour or more if they had to climb to higher altitudes to find clearer skies. There were forty-four Bomb Groups in an area the size of Vermont looking for their places. All the bombers taking off, in the right weather, could form a solid condensation trail over East Anglia. The contrails thickened into "a blanketing fuzz that makes your heart pound like hell," said one pilot. "At times you're flying totally blind and you know that in one of those blind moments you may crash into a friend." There were close calls, rough rides through the turbulence from propwash, and midair collisions. Weather reports that were often wrong left pilots in heavily overloaded bombers, with little training to fly on instruments, in gray "soupy" skies crowded with other heavy bombers. The Eighth Air Force lost three hundred bombers, 5 percent of its losses, getting into formation, far from battle.

Each B-24 group had its own assembly ship, a garishly painted, "war-weary" bomber, that served as a rallying point. The one for the 453rd was painted in a can't-miss-it checkerboard pattern. Some crews called these ships "Judas Goats" for leading them to slaughter.

The assembly ship fired flares to signal its group. Radio silence was observed. The Germans could detect the bombers two-and-a-half hours before they even reached the enemy coast.

The bombers joined by threes, then by squadrons, groups, and wings. Before they crossed the Channel or the North Sea they were flying in their division. On the ground, the English were reassured by the sight and thrumming sound of the heavy bombers passing overhead by the hundreds. "We called those boys 'our boys' and their ships 'our ships,'" said a Framlingham farm girl, whose family farm was partially taken over by a new airfield. "When those boys were returning from a raid we never felt at ease until all of them had landed."

Mid-Channel, the bombardier told the gunners to test their guns, and the fuse pins were removed to arm the bombs. At ten thousand feet the crew put on their oxygen masks and plugged in their electrically heated flight suits. They were headed to battle, and even with all the planning and briefing, the crews were left to improvise in the air. They might be with hundreds of other bombers, but they were on their own.

The night before a mission Lt. Bernard Hutain, pilot of the B-24 *Werewolf* in the 446th BG, slept fitfully before he was woken up in the cold, dark barracks to get dressed, and walk to the chow line. After that Hutain had to take "that horrible truck ride to the briefing room. Horrible to me because as a farm boy I had seen my father load cattle or pigs on a truck and take them to the slaughterhouse. Every time I got in that truck I felt just like I was one of those animals being taken out to be killed."

"The doors to the bomb bays close behind you, and you know that you are a prisoner of this ship," said a reluctant reporter for *Yank*, the Army's weekly magazine. "That imprisonment can be broken only by three factors, and they are in order: Disaster by explosion and parachuting to another prison, death, or a safe return."

This was the life my father lived as a teenager—up at 3:00 a.m., breakfast by 4:00, a briefing at the plane to get the target for the day, long hours in flight, the Luftwaffe sometimes attacking, flying through flak over the target, watching the bombs drop, flying home through more flak and possible fighter attacks, landing to be met by the Red Cross girls with sandwiches, doughnuts, and coffee, and then a shot of whiskey at the "interrogation," the debriefing. And up again to do it the next day.

## ISLE DE CAZEMBRE

The 453rd succeeded on its next mission, the August 13 bombing of a channel island, Isle de Cazembre, three miles off the coast of Brittany, where the German Navy had set up six large 194mm guns, arrayed in a circle. Each gun had a range of more than three miles. Two months after D-Day, they were firing inland at Allied troops. Carrying four of the largest available bombs, two-thousand pounds each, the *Mary Harriet* flew about a mile lower than usual, at 15,000 feet, and with sixty-eight other B-24s, obliterated the small island. "Results—Island sunk," my father noted. It was, says an account by the 453rd, "one of the finest examples of direct air support." The bombing was considered accurate: 63 percent of the bombs hit within five hundred feet and 82 percent within one thousand feet of the target. Two days later, the Germans holding the nearby port of St. Malo surrendered, followed two weeks later by the surrender of several hundred German soldiers on the island.

The *Mary Harriet's* accurate bombing would not be commended. "Crew highly P.O.," he wrote, "No ratings!" But six days later the *Mary Harriet's* squadron, the 733rd, received a citation for "distinguished and outstanding performance of duty during the period 9 May 1944 to 17 August 1944." The 733rd had flown eighty-two missions, attacking Germany twenty-six times and fifty-six targets in the occupied countries

*dropping over 1,400 tons of bombs against vital enemy installations thereby contributing materially to the success of the aerial war. Many of these missions were accomplished in the face of intense anti-aircraft fire and formidable fighter opposition. The tenacity of purpose, efficiency, determination, and devotion to duty displayed by both the ground and combat personnel of the 733rd Bombardment Squadron reflect the greatest credit upon themselves and the armed forces of the United States—By command of Major General Kepner.*

More than 1,200 bombers were attacking other coastal guns and "transportation choke points between Le Havre and Paris" that day. Seven B-17s and five B-24s were shot down. This would show up in the reports as a 1 percent loss, a deceivingly small number until you realized that this meant that one hundred-and-twenty-eight men, killed, missing, or wounded, wouldn't be returning to their barracks.

## THE PRODUCTION OF DESTRUCTION

The bombing of Europe in World War II was born in the trenches of the First World War. The horrors of poison gases—mustard, chlorine, phosgene, and tear gas—spilling into the trenches hung over the inter-war years. The English feared being gassed from above by a Zeppelin attack in the next war. The German Zeppelin and Gotha bomber raids (with explosives, not gas) on English cities were seen as a forecast of catastrophes to come. There was a raft of books in the 1920s and 1930s prophesying gas attacks from the air, panic in the streets, and worker uprisings, all leading to the end of English civilization as it was known. As war appeared near in 1938, the English government issued 35 million gas masks, which everyone, including school children, carried with them.

The bombing of England in the Great War has largely been forgotten. I knew a woman living her last years in our small town, who, as a child, had witnessed the bombing of her city, Hull, by a Zeppelin. She watched as it was shot down, exploding in flames. She was nine years old. It was terrifying—a scene from science fiction. In her nineties, she found the fireworks on the Fourth of July upsetting.

Throughout the 1930s, the partisans of air power promised that the next war would be won in the sky. There would be no trenches, no soldiers on the ground except to march into the capital city as conquerors. The RAF and a small group of U.S. Army war planners believed in the bomber. "The bomber will always get through," said Stanley Baldwin, who served three times as prime minister. The American group was so fervent they came to be known as the "Bomber Mafia." The RAF believed in going on the offensive, not spending money on defensive fighters and patrols. A bomber attack would smash the will of the enemy. One bomb had a multiplier effect of twenty in the disruption and fear it brought on, or so they claimed. After a devastating first strike, frightened civilians would sue for peace. Victory would be swift.

The theories of air supremacy promoted in the 1930s were shredded in the first battles of World War II. On the RAF's first bombing raid, by day, in Germany's Ruhr Valley, their bombs fell so far off target that German intelligence officers couldn't tell what they were trying to hit. Only 10 percent of the RAF's first night-raiding bombers were able to drop bombs within five miles of the targeted factories, and it was even worse on hazy nights lacking "a bomber's moon." The first years of the Air War, starting in 1940, were ineffective.

The RAF changed course, targeting cities, aiming to "break the spirit" of German workers. They pursued a policy of "dehousing." One ton of bombs, Churchill's chief scientific adviser, Lord Cherwell, claimed, would destroy twenty to forty houses, leaving one hundred to two hundred people homeless. They turned to "area bombing," to annihilating cities in firestorms, burning Hamburg first—16,000 buildings set ablaze at once. The total number killed in that "hurricane of fire" is unknown; 45,000 corpses were found in the rubble. One million lost their homes. The RAF took the code name for their attack from one of the biblical cities destroyed by a rain of sulfur and fire—Operation Gomorrah. The RAF wasn't bombing armies or factories, but the civilians who supported them.

The Americans arrived with great claims: They would bomb with "precision" by day; they would only bomb military targets and they would fly without fighter protection. They would shoot the enemy out of sky, downing "two to three fighters for every bomber lost." With the Norden bombsight they said they could drop a bomb into a pickle barrel from 30,000 feet. Their war plans were more "a matter of faith than of knowledge," says the Air Force's own official history.

General Ira Eaker landed in England in 1942 with not even enough men to field a baseball team. He had a staff of six and no airplanes. Two years later he was in charge of 185,000 pilots, crew, and support staff, with four thousand airplanes—an operation that was two-thirds the size of America's largest corporation, General Motors.

They got into battle in 1943 before they were ready, but needing a victory for the headlines to show the British that they were there to win the war. They attempted "precision daylight bombing." They attempted to fly without fighter escort. It worked in the first raid on Rouen and came to grief soon after with many causalities.

The early Air War was an experiment. The Air Force had navigators who couldn't navigate, gunners shooting all over the sky, hitting their own airplanes, and bombardiers who couldn't bomb—only 10 to 15 percent of the bombs were falling within one thousand feet of the target. The top-secret Norden bombsight, one of the most expensive projects of the war, was hard to use in battle. It required many calculations and a level-flying plane; it required perfect, non-battle conditions. But it was brilliantly promoted.

Q: Can you really put a bomb in a pickle barrel?

A: Which pickle would you like to hit? said its inventor, Carl Norden.

The early missions were "suicide missions," say historians. The Allies were losing the Air War. The Eighth Air Force "is not a credit to the American Army," Gen. Eaker reported to his superiors in 1943. It is "an unkept promise," he said. They had turned things around by the time my father arrived a year later. The Air War grew in its ferocity. The Americans abandoned "precision" for a wider bombing pattern, and bombing "blind" through the clouds (with radar), and, in 1945, attacking Berlin. The Eighth Air Force had success bombing railroad yards, factories, and oil depots—now, close to half of its bombs were falling within one thousand feet of the target, and 80 percent within two thousand feet—but the RAF kept to an aggressive city-wrecking campaign. "Terror bombing," the critics called it.

It took a long time for the technology of bombing to teach its practitioners. They needed fighter escorts, and they needed the fighters set free to attack, to dive down and strafe waiting aircraft, a lesson that took a change in command later in the war.

Bringing the war to the sky was promoted as a technological wonder that would obsolete the battlefield. It would shorten wars and ultimately save lives. But the Bomber War wasn't a *deus ex machina*, a magic act to free armies from bloody fighting. It was not sudden or decisive. It was not precise; it did not end wars in days or weeks. It was grinding, repetitive, hitting the same targets again and again with severe losses on some missions. The Eighth Air Force struggled mightily to drop their bombs on target. It came down to numbers, to the 350,000 men who would serve in the Eighth Air Force, to the more than 603,000 sorties—individual flights—by bombers and fighters, to the 697,000 tons of bombs dropped. In the end, the Air War, like trench warfare, was a war of attrition. "American Air Force publicists lauded the surgical precision of the raids . . . but the German economy was bludgeoned to death by the blunt instrument of saturation bombing," says historian Donald L. Miller.

Aerial combat was the opposite of having unmoving armies dug in for years, but it, too, was an industrial monotony producing destruction. This is what I learned that night in Wales when I saw *Target for Tonight*: the routine grind, the assembly-line job of bombing your enemy. The production of destruction is run like a business.

The Bomber War was, as one of its proponents claimed, General William Tecumseh Sherman brought into the twentieth century. Every citizen, every rail line and factory, was on the front line. But the Bomber War—the burning of London, Munich, Coventry, Hamburg, Dresden, and close to one hundred other cities in England and Germany—made Sherman's March look docile.

Military historians, making the obvious visible, say that most bullets miss. But the proponents of the Air War promoted it as warfare in which all the bullets kill. They oversold the Air War and would be judged for it after the war.

While my father was keeping track of his missions, along with many other guys who kept their own "forbidden dairies," the Air Force was working around the clock, analyzing the day's missions to plan the next ones, trying to tell a story.

In the air, the Eighth Air Force flew in formation, found its target, and dropped bombs. On the ground, the Air Force told stories. It was a narrative-making machine with a legion of men and women typing, analyzing photos, sending reports up the chain of command, typing their way to victory as if it was a typewriter war.

Each mission was a story, one to be studied and assessed. Each mission was a chapter in the book that would tell how the Eighth Air Force was essential to win the war.

I've read through thousands of pages of mission plans, jumbles of letters and code names for targeted cities all in capital letters, rows of data for take-off times, radio frequencies for "bunchers" and "splashers" to gather the bombers into flying formations, times for crossing the coast, times to arrive over the target, tonnage dropped, returning altitudes, route maps and maps of the deviations from the routes, planes sent, planes lost, photos of smoke rising from the bombing, and assessments of the damage. These represent a bombing mission, rows of numbers and the jibber jabber of code names looking like the rows of graves at Arlington. So much effort to see, to understand what they were doing.

Summarizing the results, in the reports I reviewed, they were reluctant to use the word "poor"—"fair," "fair to good," but seldom "poor." The evaluations change, sometimes from the preliminary report to the interpretation of the bombing photos, and sometimes as the results move up the chain of command—"poor" falling out of the report in favor of "fair to good" and "good." "Excellent" is seldom used, perhaps because that would call too much attention to itself.

This is an organization looking for a story with a beginning, middle, and ending. We sent out 1,100 bombers and 630 fighters to Manz, Frankfurt, Ulm. We sent them to bomb synthetic oil plants, fuel depots, airplane factories, and railroad marshaling yards. And what happened? Did it work? Did it bring us closer to victory?

The reports tell of the relentlessness of war, the industrial side of trying to perfect the logistics of destruction. Each month, it seemed, Gen. Eaker or Gen. Arnold promised *New! Improved!* destruction. They promised their superiors and their British allies, and they talked it up among their own airmen. *Target Victory*, published by the Eighth's 2nd Air Division, was like any other company newsletter praising employees and touting new products, but the good news announced, "a truly great bombing week" and the headlines highlighted the bombs that fell on target—"New High in August! 2nd Wing Leads Scoring Analysis"—and the biggest "hits"—"Best Hit by a Group This Week: 389th Tops Scoring on Karlsruhe" with photos showing smoke steaming from the "strike point." Throughout the newsletter, bombs are the key graphic element, used as the bars in bar charts comparing the accuracy of different bomber groups. "You can shake the hand of the nearest crew member for we hit the jackpot of bombing precision . . . the most accurate month in [our] history."

Even as the reports note the loss of bombers, the damage and causalities, the power of the war is diluted. This is the war's scorecard, not the war. This isn't the war's true cost. The war is already disappearing in the reports, even as the crewmen, back in their sacks, sleep deeply, or fitfully, reliving the day's mission in their dreams.

The bombers didn't win the war, but in 1944 the Air Force choked off the railroads and the coal that powered almost all of Germany, shut down oil production, and stifled the Luftwaffe before D-Day. After years of aerial combat, the Luftwaffe was running out of experienced pilots, fuel, and airplanes. The Army Air Forces left a troubling, mixed record.

With the surprise attack of the Battle of the Bulge, from mid-December 1944 to mid-January, the Allies began to get desperate. More V1s and V2s were hitting London, one wiping out a Woolworths crowded with Christmas shoppers. Bigger rockets might follow. The Nazis were working on the A-9/A-10 "America Project," an ICBM aimed at New York City. And there were many reports that the Nazis were racing to build the first atomic bomb.

Germany would fall, but when? In January 1945, one possibility was that the war could run on until November. But there was a whole other war to win; men and planes were needed in the Pacific.

The Eighth hit cities when it targeted marshaling yards. The Russians were pressing from the East. The Allies wanted to disrupt rail traffic and cause chaos. They bombed the center of Berlin. The head of the Eighth Air Force objected. The city was packed with refugees. The Air Force bombed the railyards of Dresden; the RAF destroyed the city. Stalin requested that. A terrible inferno consumed Dresden.

After the war, very few wanted to sort out the Air Wars. The British chose the heroic story of the Spitfire pilots holding off the Luftwaffe in the Battle of Britain, as memorialized in Churchill's famous speech: "Never in the field of human conflict was so much owed by so many to so few." Churchill never made a speech about the brave crews of Bomber Command. Nearly seventy years passed before a monument was dedicated in London to the bomber crews. In America, the war's brutality was lost in the bright lights of praise for "The Good War."

## OLDENBURG AND DESSAU

He considered his next mission, on August 15, a "milk run"—Air Force talk for any mission that held as much danger as a milkman saw on his delivery route. There was no flak and no enemy fighters. This was his sixth mission, but only the fifth that would count for his combat tour. The *Mary Harriet* took part in attacking an airfield nine miles northwest of Oldenburg, Germany. A history of the 453rd says the airfield was "well hit" with 78 percent of the bombs falling within one thousand feet of the aiming point. But he wrote that the *Mary Harriet's* bombs "fell short and hit runway."

With his fifth mission, he was awarded the Air Medal for "meritorious achievement." The Air Medal was awarded to all airmen who had flown five missions against the enemy.

He had a rougher time the next day, August 16. It was a long mission. They flew deep into Germany at 25,000 feet. He was on oxygen for six hours. Attacking a Junkers aero engine plant in Dessau, one of the leading planes was hit by flak, throwing off the rest of the squadron. The Eighth Air Force "bombed on lead"—the other aircraft released their bombs when the lead bombardier did. The deputy-lead bomber, flying in the low-left position, was "far short of the target" when it "suffered a direct hit" that caused its bombs to accidentally release, says a history of the 453rd. The rest of the squadron took this as their cue, and thirty tons of bombs missed the engine factory. Another malfunction followed. The leader flying in the high-right position had a "bombsight failure," and another thirty tons of high explosives fell short. The *Mary Harriet's* bombs missed. The rest of the force of ninety-nine B-24s hit the scattered buildings of the engine and airframe factory, which were dispersed in more than fifty workshops and hangars around an airfield. The assembly shops at the east end of the airfield were painted to look as if they had already been bombed. Eight weeks later, Dessau was repaired.

The Luftwaffe was "aggressive" attacking the bombers with more than ninety Fw 190s and Me 109s, says a mission report. There is "a marked increase in German fighter opposition," said Eighth Air Force Fighter Command. "It is apparent that the enemy has been able to recuperate and rebuild his defensive fighter strength.... Future deep strategic attacks will possibly be faced with increasingly heavier opposition," making it "more difficult" to escort large formations. Ten B-17s "were seen to go down during combat." In all, that day, twenty-three bombers and three fighters were shot down.

Second Lt. Milton A. Stanchfield's B-24, *Flying Bull,* from the 453rd, didn't make it to Dessau. The *Flying Bull* was shot down by fighters. Stanchfield held his plane level while his crew bailed out; he didn't trust parachutes. He'd take his chances crash landing. Seriously injured, he was taken to a hospital where he died that day. His right waist gunner also didn't jump. He was either wounded or had passed out from a lack of oxygen. His copilot could not find his parachute. He jumped by hanging on to the back of the left waist gunner, who wore the standard belly-pack parachute. They surrendered to an angry mob who turned them over to three SS officers. The officers drove them into a nearby forest and shot both men in the back of the head. The five remaining crewmen parachuted seventy-eight miles west of Dessau and were taken prisoner. They would wait for the war's end in Stalag Luft 3 and Stalag Luft 4.

On that day's mission, 239 men were killed, missing, or wounded. The *Flying Bull's* pilot, Lt. Stanchfield, was just one of the day's dead in a long war that would kill, by some estimates, 55 million people. He was twenty-two years old and married. He would be missing a long time from his family's life. His older brother Albert would live to be eighty-two, and his younger brother Richard until he was seventy-seven. His wife Arlene would live to be eighty-five. Milton A. Stanchfield is buried in the American Cemetery in the Netherlands, Plot D, Row 4, Grave 30.

From his open window on the war, my father reported that "8 Me 109s attacked stragglers." The P-51s escorting his force of bombers reported that they "engaged about twenty Me 109s," destroying more than half of them. The flak was "intense—amazingly accurate," he wrote. There were two flak holes in the *Mary Harriet*. He added, "Today I said, 'Manny, you've had it!'" Manny is what some customers at the luncheonette used to call his father, and it's a nickname that he would be known by at work in the years to come.

## A Roster of the Lost

On November 9, 1944, Lt. John "Jack" Friedhaber's crew posed for a photo by their plane, *Never Mrs,* one of the B-24s based at Old Buckenham. Two days later they were killed, shot down by antiaircraft guns over a synthetic oil factory in Bottrop, Germany. Hit by flak just before dropping its bombs, *Never Mrs* caught fire, the plane pitching into a dive, a wing coming off before it crashed.

This was a common story. I have looked at too many photos of crews lining up like a small sports team of ten in front of their B-24, each man searching for a pose—casual/assured, heroic/assured, hanging around/assured—each maybe thinking that this could be his last photo on earth. It's like a yearbook in which the soon-to-die and the most-likely-to-succeed are side by side. These photos grant us an eerie omniscience. There's the crew of the *Lucky Penny* who you know will be killed on May 8, 1944. They will be hit by attacking fighters. The number three engine will catch fire and the fire will spread, exploding the *Lucky Penny*, which will crash at Feldmark Buhne, Germany. There's Lt. Milton A. Stanchfield and his crew standing before the charging *Flying Bull* painted on the nose of their bomber. They have only nine days to live.

There are page after page of photos. It's all too much, this procession in which youth and death are entwined, caught in some kind of random, coin-flipping experiment. The men of *Shack Rabbit II, Choo Choo Baby, Worry Bird* . . . lost—and lost is the most commonly used word, as if they had just disappeared. The words "killed" or "dead" are seldom used. "Lost" leaves the door open—they could be down at sea, parachuting into France or Holland. Lost airmen did rise again sometimes. Hidden by the French resistance, spirited through France, crossing the Channel somehow, and then walking into the mess at the airfield. Back, perhaps a little "strange," as they might say, and celebrated, crossing over from lost to lucky.

In the yearbook-like photos the men and their flying machines are still intact. But there are also many crash photos: B-24s nosed into the earth, belly to the ground looking like something that never could have flown; B-24s in heaps and twists of jagged metal; B-24s ablaze, a torrent of fire and smoke. *Shamrock* smashed hard into the earth, in small pieces. Your eye searches for patterns—is that a wing, is that a tail, part of the fuselage? *Lucky Lucky* with its severed tail lying on the ground. An unnamed bomber hit by flak: a line torn through a wing as if high-flying metal termites had bored a path or a can opener had pried the plane's skin apart. *Queenie Witchcraft II* landing with the glass shot out of the tail gunner turret and the tail gunner dead. Another landing with its nose turret blown apart beyond recognition, and another with the ball turret—the one hanging from the belly of the plane—smashed as the bomber is forced to make a wheels-up landing, sliding down the runway, killing the ball turret gunner as the waiting officers, gathered to "sweat them in," could only watch.

The roster of the lost in just the 453rd is long:

Lost in the first six months of 1944, shot down, forced down in Switzerland, or damaged never to fly again: *Cee Gee, Little Agnes, Little Mike, Briney Marlin, Yankee Doll, Ginnie, Rumpelstiltskin, Ken O Kay, Libby Raider, Lillie Belle, Betty Boop, Shack Rabbit, Portland Annie, Little Bryan, Shack Rabbit II, Cabin the Sky, Little Joe, Lil Eight Ball, Rooster, Black Jed, "663," Ken O Kay II, Blondes Away, Cee Gee II, Borsuk's Bitch, Valkyrie,*

*Pete, Gypsy Queen, Pug, Lucky Penny, Choo Choo Baby, Mackey, Sunshine, The Golden Gaboon, Notre Dame, Zeus, Becky, War Bride, Archibald, Begin the Beguine,* and *Pay Day.*

Lost while my father was serving at Old Buc from July to October 1944: *Jabber Wock!, Battle Package, Stolen Moments, Our Baby, Diana-Mite, Hard to Get, Strickly Business, Flying Bull, Hoo-Jive, Flak Hack, Porky, Sleepy Time Gal, Old Butch, Shack Happy,* and *Lucky Penny II.*

Another thirty bombers would be lost in the closing five-and-a-half months of the war in Europe. The 453rd started operating in February 1944 with sixty-one bombers; by V-E Day only one of the originals remained. In World War II, 366 airmen died while serving in the 453rd Bombardment Group at Old Buckenham.

Here's a small part of the roster of the lost (and sometimes the lucky):

There's *The Golden Gaboon* and crew in one photo. In the next photo the plane is burning up on the main runway, thick coils of gray-black smoke, as men rush toward it. *The Golden Gaboon* was returning all shot up on May 30, 1944, when it was caught in the slipstream of the preceding plane and crashed. The crew escaped.

*Zeus* was the next plane to land, flying home at low altitude on only two engines—and one working landing gear—to find the runway blocked by the burning bomber. The pilot, Lt. Lester J. Baer, was forced to a short alternate runway, landing in a strong crosswind. Everyone watched as the one working wheel touched down and the plane rolled until the left wing-tip dipped and the number one propeller caught the ground, swinging *Zeus* around as it came to a stop in a cloud of dust. The crew walked away and Lt. Baer was awarded the Distinguished Flying Cross. It was "the most skillful crosswind landing that Old Buc has ever seen," says a history of the 453rd.

There's *El Flako*, hit by flak behind the bomb bay over Dortmund, Germany on November 2, 1944. The wings, main body, and the tail came down miles apart. *El Flako* was a "lucky" plane, having flown seventy-seven missions, but this was the first mission for its new crew. Only two managed to bail out. They were captured by a farmer and shot dead. ("Please don't shoot!"—*Bitte nicht schießen!*—was the only German my father ever learned, and he never forgot it.)

The schoolboys who lived nearby loved the crew of *El Flako*. When John Symonds was ten years old he would go after school with his friends to talk to the crew after their missions—school got out about the time the bombers were usually returning. They conducted their own schoolboy debriefing. The day their favorite didn't return, the boys cycled home "terribly sad." Many years later, when Symonds was visiting relatives in Holland, he happened to meet someone who put him in touch with a German historian who took him to the crash site. They dug up some fragments and Symonds brought them back to the museum at Old Buc. "Now she's come back home," he said.

There's the unnamed B-24, piloted by Lt. Roscoe C. Brown, which rose only a few feet before crashing on December 27, 1944. Brown, the commander with the radar that would guide the bombing, was the first to take off. The runway was icy—straw had been spread to add traction—and, unknown to Brown, his wings had iced over. The bomber crashed at the end of the runway, tearing off the tail, which was on fire with the tail gunner inside. The two waist gunners jumped clear and pulled the tail gunner out, snuffing out his flaming clothes. The ammo on board began to go off, followed by the bombs, destroying the wreck. The fire trucks and ambulance crews could only stand by. Lt. Brown and five of his crew were killed. The 453rd canceled that day's mission.

There's the *Spirit of Notre Dame*, which collided mid-air with *Worry Bird* on February 9, 1945, on their way back from Magdeburg, Germany. Both planes continued to fly, but on its final approach *Worry Bird* crashed "one hundred yards from the runway in full view of all those who came to 'sweat them in.'" The entire crew was killed.

There's *Star Eyes*. On April 10, 1945, the day before the 453rd flew its last mission, *Star Eyes*, over Wittenberg, Germany, took a direct hit, broke in two and blew up, the airplane's tail falling separately to earth. The war was over for the ten men aboard. Their death was as final as if it had happened six or twelve months earlier, but its timing seems cruel. They were just weeks away from the rest of their lives. No one wants to be the last one killed in a war. "The extra day of war could be your unlucky one," said an Air Force newsletter. "Surely it will be for some of your buddies."

The bombers fell out of the sky many "different ways," recalled Lt. Hal Turrell, a navigator and bombardier in the 445th BG. "Sometimes they will slide down tail-first and be completely covered in flames. Some will go into a flat spin; the plane revolves around its nose. Others go into a tailspin; the wings revolve around the fuselage. Sometimes they tumbled end over end with parts breaking off and flying in all directions. Others with no visible damage would circle in a descending pattern. Some dived straight into the ground."

Sometimes the planes would blow up, the bombs aboard exploding, or the fuel in the tanks, or both. "First there is a brief white flash that quickly turns into a great red fireball. The aircraft splits into hundreds of pieces of metal, some with a slight hint of their previous function, such as a wing. . . . You might see bodies, not ever parachutes," said Turrell. With five thousand pounds of bombs and thousands of gallons of fuel, an exploding bomber launched shards of metal, torn up wings, hatch covers, and the limbs and smashed bodies of their fellow airmen. Men, pinned to the walls and floor by the centrifugal force of a spinning plane, had little time to escape before the bomber hit the ground. If they could jump, they might be swept by the slipstream into the tail and crushed. The crews in other bombers could only watch as men fell five miles down through bombers and fighters in battle, fell without a parachute or with a parachute on fire, or were machine gunned to death as they hung from a parachute.

It happened in an instant, or it happened for hours, and if you landed, you had to walk away from the memory of it so you could fly the next day. Or it happened just like this: "I noted a flash of light out of the corner of my right eye," said Lt. Roy Test, pilot of the B-17 *Bad Penny*. "The plane that had been flying right next to us had exploded and simply disappeared." Ten men, eighteen tons of aluminum, with tons more of high explosives and fuel: Gone.

As a navigator, Turrell was supposed to keep a log of what he saw: the fighter attacks, the ones they may have shot down, the other bombers going down, if any parachutes were seen. After the flak and fighter attacks, "I looked at my log and realized I had entered very little after the first shot. I now know what was meant by the shock and fog of battle. There is nothing that can prepare you for it. Suddenly you realize you are mortal. I then felt there was no chance I would survive to complete my tour," he said. This was his first combat mission. He would fly twenty-nine more.

Captain Michael Benarick, who piloted *Rumpelstiltskin* in the 453rd, wrote home to his mother: "The planes . . . falling out of the sky reminded me of the falling leaves from the tree in our backyard in early fall. These leaves had men in them. I prayed a lot that day. I know that helped."

The stories pile up, canceling each other out, the way colors in the spectrum create white light. Story after story of good men blown away in an instant, of the chaos of moments—shrapnel and fire inside the plane, men passing out from loss of oxygen, planes shredded in the sky, men drowning in ditched and sinking planes, men bleeding, decapitated, maimed, men crying, breaking down. One crewman from the 467th BG in a crippled bomber was ordered to throw the dead body of his friend overboard because everything that wasn't bolted down had to go if they were to make it home.

"Training in the states nowhere prepared you for the slaughter of the first mission. It was like someone slashing at you with a big knife," said Sgt. Hank Hall, a waist gunner on *Ack Ack Annie* from the 91st BG.

"Combat is hard to catch in words. You say, maybe, 20 mm shells smashed the turret, ripped through the fuselage. But no phrase will tell the empty five seconds in the guts of every man aboard as they waited and even felt to know whether that had been *the* attack," wrote Hutton and Rooney.

*Or you say, fire began to glow within the engine nacelle and eat slowly back into the wing, and no words you can own measure the limitless courage it takes for men in that plane to watch flame consume the very thing which bears them aloft yet struggle not just to live but to strike back. . . . Such times are of the mind and the viscera, and speak an infinite horror; you can tell little of them.*

Some planes returned smeared inside with blood and vomit. On landing, the Red Cross girls would greet the fliers with coffee and donuts, but sometimes, still keyed up from the flight, the men would vomit it all back up.

These young Americans out there on the table-flat land of East Anglia were history's momentary apparition—young men fighting a new kind of war. They could be gone in a moment, their names wiped off the chalkboard listing the crews, their bunks stripped, and a few of their possessions "vultured" by their bunk mates and the rest sent home. Their last letter might be the one they left with someone they deemed to be "lucky"—luck was a coveted attribute. When Napoleon was reviewing a list of men recommended for promotion, next to a man's name he'd write, "Is he lucky?" There were lucky men and lucky aircraft.

"I guess we were carrying a horseshoe today," said Lt. John W Hargrove, a B-17 bombardier. "The plane flying off our wing not more than one hundred feet from us was hit by flak and punctured like a salt shaker while we landed without a hole in our plane." In "thirty-four missions not one of our crew has been scratched," said Sgt. Frank E. Sawin, Jr., a B-17 radio operator, "but today, on our thirty-fifth attack, a hunk of heavy flak hit the left waist gunner in the knee, but not seriously. I still think we're a lucky crew." The official stories celebrate courage and bravery; the men talked about luck.

We can't ask more of our men, said Gen. Eaker. Two missions ago, he said, "We sent out one thousand combat crew members and lost one hundred of them, killed, wounded, or missing. It is quite evident, therefore, that a combat crew must be very good or very lucky to complete an operational tour."

A combat tour was a mix of tedium and danger, of routine and horror, of missions where nothing happens and missions where the world comes apart and the end comes. It was an "invariable round of work, sleep, death," as one biographer wrote. The breakfasts in the dark before a mission, eggs on the plate, the stony silence, the nail-polish remover smell of explosives and piss and smoke in the bomber, the men joking with one another, the long drumming hours in the air, death below, death in the sky. A pass for three days of leave and dances and Red Cross girls and more girls. You're at the start of your life; you're maybe at the end of your life. Fear and bore-dom, fear and courage, fear and some stupid Army order.

The histories of the bomber groups are a march of men who were loved, smart, prepared, young, and gone in a moment; and men who were grumpy, ill-prepared, young, and gone, too, in a moment. You're nineteen, twenty, twenty-one, and this is all you'll see of life: Your hometown, Army training, East Anglia, the sky, the end.

The bombers fell; men were killed or were missing. Men completed their tours. Other men, other crews and planes, arrived. And the war went on.

## METZ

On August 18, my father flew in a different B-24, *My Babs*, to bomb an airfield in Metz, France. Initially, Winston Churchill had opposed bomb-ing occupied France. The "slaughter" of French civilians might "leave a legacy of hate" and "smear the good name of the Royal Air Force across the world," he told Franklin Roosevelt. "It must be remembered, on the one hand, that this slaughter is among a friendly people who have com-mitted no crimes against us, and not among the German foe, with their record of cruelty and ruthlessness." In Germany, Churchill was commit-ted to a policy of "dehousing," of bombing civilians out of their homes, a policy that led to the firestorms in Hamburg, Dresden, and dozens of other cities killing a half million or more and leaving five million without homes. In France, Churchill sought assurances that no more than one hundred French would be killed in each attack. He finally agreed that transportation should be targeted in France.

General Carl "Tooey" Spaatz, the commander of the Strategic Air Forces in Europe, was also wary of bombing railroads, bridges, and air-fields in France. He was worried that the Germans would exaggerate the civilian causalities for their propaganda. He set restrictions, banning bombing with radar through cloud cover. "Blind bombing," as the airmen called it, killed thousands of civilians. Only two percent of the bombs hit within one thousand feet of the aiming point.

The raid on the Metz airfield confirms Churchill's objections: some of the bombs fell ten miles short. "Takeoff delayed by runaway turbo," my father reported. "Bombs dropped 10 miles short of target due to error of deputy lead. 3 other planes dropped."

The bombs from the deputy lead, and the three other B-24s, fell ten miles short, but where? In three hundred pages of mission plans, reports, and intelligence assessments, I find no mention of this. The results of bombing the Metz airfield by the 453rd are rated as "good," with one squadron reporting 92 percent of their bombs landing within one thousand feet of the target's bull's-eye, and another claiming 100 percent. The airfield was a "mass of smoke & flames," my father wrote.

To pick out one errant bomber makes it sound as if this was an isolated event on a fine summer's day, with twelve tons of high explosives from four B-24s breaking the peace and falling on a village or a farm—a "Flub-Dub Blitz" or "summer plowing," as they called such mistakes. But that day over Metz, there were seventy-eight B-24s dropping 234 tons of bombs on the airfield. And this was just a part of the 772 bombers and hundreds of fighters dispatched to fifteen assigned targets plus a few "targets of opportunity" they picked up along the way.

"Hundreds of U.S. Eighth Air Force P-47 Thunderbolts, P-38 Lightnings, and P-51 Mustangs swarmed down to bomb and strafe rail lines, highways, and airfields in France Friday, hampering escape or reinforcement of the hard-pressed Germany armies," said a press release from the headquarters of the United States Strategic Air Forces in Europe.

*The low-level fighter attacks left in their wake a huge toll of destruction," said another report, this one from public relations at the Eighth Air Force. "Forty-seven oil tank cars and seventy-two other railway cars were damaged or destroyed, thirty-eight locomotives disabled, two hundred and twenty trucks and highway vehicles were shot up and fifty-one grounded aircraft were destroyed. . . . Twenty-one of our fighters are missing from the day's operations.*

Further from Metz, near Paris,

*several hundred German foot soldiers were caught in the low-level attack fifteen miles west of Compiegne. The Mustangs were strafing a military train of six cars parked near a field when they found about five hundred soldiers deployed on a nearby field.*

*"They seemed to be going through some kind of maneuvers, for they were lying down in groups of about six," said First Lieutenant William S. Pennell, of Gilmer, Texas. "As we came down to make a pass at them, some of them got up and made a run for cover. We machine-gunned them and then came back and made another pass. In all, we must have gotten about 200 of them."*

*American troops were reported entering the outskirts of Paris by one of the Mustang pilots. . . . "You should see the road leading to Paris; they are just a mass of American troops. They waved to me as I went over," said Second Lieutenant Donald S. Perkins, of Palos Park, Ill., a Mustang pilot.*

This is only a partial accounting of the bombs and bullets set loose over part of France on that August day. The confidential report from the headquarters of the Eighth Fighter Command runs for eleven closely typed pages.

The 453rd, flying with the 2nd Air Division, crossed the channel over Brighton flying south about one hundred miles until they turned east near Laval, France, and flew on a course south of Paris for 250 miles, where the force divided for their assignments in Pacy-sur-Armancon, St. Dizier, Nancy, and Metz. Somewhere, ten miles to the southwest of Metz, assuming they were on course, the war fell on some part of France, but there is no record except for the notes of a gunner flying on *My Babs.*

At last, I could account for the mistake. The Group Commanders met regularly at the headquarters of the 2nd Combat Wing to critique the missions. They reviewed the performance of the bombers at Metz. The review was led by Col. Milton W. Arnold, commanding officer of the 2nd Combat Wing, and Lt. Col. James M. Stewart, Chief of Staff. (Movie star Jimmy Stewart to his many fans.)

On the August 18 run to Metz, Arnold was flying as the wing commander leading the attack with the 389th Bomb Group. Two other bomb groups flew with the 389th—the 453rd to the right and 445th trailing by one minute to the high right.

"Good runs were made on the target with excellent bombing results shown," says the meeting's minutes. But: "One squadron of the 389th had an accidental premature release." The squadron isn't named.

The 389th had blundered. At other meetings, the assembled officers scrutinized mistakes. They questioned navigators, bombardiers, and lieutenants about bombers out of formation, unable to find the target, struggling back, missing important communications, arriving late at the target and rendezvous points. But Col. Arnold faced no further questions.

## WISMAR AND BASDORF

In the summer of 1944, the Eighth Air Force was flying missions at a relentless pace. It was a summer of bad weather, but they flew almost every day—twenty-eight days in June, twenty-seven in July, and twenty-three in August. The losses, too, were relentless. The Eighth lost half of its strength—1,022 heavy bombers—and two-thirds of its 900 fighters. But their crews had a better chance of surviving their tours. The casualty rate had been cut in half since 1943. Airmen faced a 36 percent chance of being killed or captured. Each time they left England they had a one-in-three chance, on average, of not returning. That's a tidy statistic, but what they believed their chances were on any given mission no doubt fluctuated. Did a 36 percent chance really feel any different from a 75 percent chance of being shot down when a fighter was closing in on you at six miles a minute?

The reduced rate was due, in part, to Maj. Jimmy Doolittle, a hero for leading the daring raid on Tokyo early in the war. He took over the Eighth in January 1944 and set the fighters free to take the offensive. They were no longer pinned to the bombers. "We used to call our fighters 'pursuit' planes between wars, and that was what they were supposed to do—pursue the enemy," Doolittle said. "This was the most important and far-reaching military decision I made during the war."

At the same time he freed his fighter planes, Doolittle encumbered his fighting men. He increased the length of a combat tour from twenty-five to thirty missions (and later to thirty-five). And the end of a tour wasn't guaranteed; airmen were only eligible to be released. Morale plummeted and would fall again when D-Day didn't bring the war to an end. "Many actually and seriously believed they would be home by Christmas of 1944," says a wartime report from the 453rd. Predictions of Hitler's fall "ran rampant." "Operations were to cease immediately, but they never did." There were "fantastic stories" making the rounds of "huge banners" hanging from the Statue of Liberty that said, "Welcome Home Eighth Air Force." But the homecoming would have to wait.

They were flying sometimes every day, facing a one-third chance of being killed or captured, the finish line had been moved twice, and the war felt like it would never end. "The air crews were sunk in pessimism; they had worked and fought to exhaustion," says historian Richard G. Davis. They were "quiet, edgy, morose." Some drank a great deal; others confessed to being numb. "I had taught myself not to feel anything at all," said Ben Smith, a radio operator on a B-17. One day he joined a volleyball game. No one shouted or laughed. "The entire game was played in silence."

A week after Metz they were sent to bomb a Dornier aircraft factory in Wismar, Germany, but they ran into engine trouble. They were not flying the *Mary Harriet*, but an older B-24—*Heavenly Body*—that had been with the 453rd since its start. "No. 3 engine feathered"—shut down—my father wrote. "Had to salvo bombs. Flew part of the mission there & all the way back on three engines. Sweated out No.2." They were close to losing a second engine.

Vail, his pilot, kept a close watch on the *Mary Harriet*, one time refusing a replacement engine because he had no faith in them. But he probably had little to say about *Heavenly Body* before they boarded for a seven-hour-long flight. *Heavenly Body* had been in for repairs that May for its battle-damaged No. 2 and No. 4 engines. That may have been why it failed.

Their next flight was a long run to Basdorf, just twelve miles from "Big B," Berlin. He was at his usual gun position and also the tail gun. The mission was recalled after they hit high clouds over Denmark and Northern Germany.

## Karlsruhe

On September 8, after a layoff of eleven days, they were sent to destroy a railroad marshaling yard in Karlsruhe, Germany. Railroad yards were singled out to break the German economy and stop troops and their supplies. From September 1944 until V-E Day eight months later, twice as many bombs fell on these key transportation points than on any other target. The railroad yards were in the center of the old cities and they were hit hard when the Eighth Air Force dropped its bombs with radar through cloud cover. "A well-bombed marshaling yard meant a well-bombed city," says historian Davis. Air Force officials strenuously avoided calling this "blind bombing."

Vail and his crew were flying *Her Man* a long way—seven hours in the air, five of those on oxygen, at 27,000 feet, carrying 2,700 gallons of fuel and ten 500-pound bombs. Results for their effort: "None," wrote my father. The mission reports say the results were "unobserved." Germany was heavily overcast. "10/10 clouds all the way," he wrote. "Lead ship took Group 25 miles off course to Ludwigshafen."

The flak was "intense and accurate," he wrote. They were hit—"about a dozen flak holes"—as were three other bombers from the 453rd. *Corky* and *Never Mrs* landed safely in France. *Flak Hack* ditched in the North Sea, more than two hundred miles northeast of Old Buckenham. Four of the crew spent seven hours in a dinghy riding out thirty-foot waves before they were picked up by an air-sea rescue speedboat. Using a small hand mirror to catch the sun they had signaled a passing bomber, which alerted the rescue boat. Five of their fellow crewmen were killed in action.

The hydraulic system on *Her Man* was "shot out." "Landed with no brakes. Engineer's eyes irritated by hydraulic fluid," he wrote. The main hydraulic system operated the brakes, flaps, landing gear, and bomb-bay doors. When landing without brakes, the training films and manuals said to tie parachutes to each machine gun support and throw the chutes out the open waist gun ports. *Her Man* was a newer B-24 with the ports enclosed with Plexiglas, so they probably didn't do this. It was also advised to have the crew move to the back of the plane to weigh down the tail.

On this day of war, the world's first long-range ballistic missile, the V-2 (the Nazi's "Vengeance Weapon Two") made its first three strikes, exploding in the suburbs of recently liberated Paris and in London, where the first rocket killed three and injured seventeen. The second took no lives.

My father's last note on this mission: "Temp −38 C. [−36.4 F] Froze two fingers."

He had frostbite, but it didn't stop him from flying. "Although I was wounded, I had my hand wrapped in a bandage. I kept my hand behind me when it came to the debriefing. I didn't want to be grounded. I'm going to finish my tour and get it over with. I didn't want to bow out, which I could do because flying is strictly voluntary. I wanted to get my part of it done."

Frostbite was the most common injury, far outnumbering combat wounds in the first war years, and this surprised the Army Air Forces, even though they were sending thousands of men to high altitudes in bombers open to the weather in conditions only seen at polar extremes and the world's highest peaks. It could fall to forty degrees below zero in a B-24, and gunners at the open windows were subject to a "windblast" that could send temperatures even lower, to 60 below zero.

Each airman was bundled up in long underwear, wool pants, fleece-lined suit, sheepskin-lined leather jacket, and a heated jumpsuit with gloves. With the parachute harness, oxygen mask and hose, flak jacket and helmet, all this weighed around twenty-five pounds, making them look like fat bears ready for hibernation. The electric suits were prone to shorting out. A short anywhere along the circuit of the heating element shut down the entire suit—a fault that was corrected in the redesigned suits available by 1944.

He also wore gunners' gloves, a heavy sheepskin mitten lined with wool that had a trigger finger, so that the glove looks almost like a cloven hoof with its odd, unexpected extra finger. It looks medieval, the kind of thing you'd see in a museum glass case. To accommodate his bad hand, he wore two different sizes, a medium on the good, right hand, and a larger one on the left hand.

Men wounded in the air, with their heated suits shot-up and useless, could end up lying on the bomber's freezing floor for hours with no medical aid but what little his fellow crewmen knew how to provide. Sometimes desperate crews, knowing they were four or five hours from home, put their injured crewmate in a parachute, put the rip cord in his hand, and sent him overboard hoping he'd find mercy once captured by the Germans. In England, on landing, the injured were carried off the plane with swollen feet, hands, and faces, frostbite that would turn purple in a day or two, then black. One third of the frostbite victims needed to be hospitalized. "This is a real emergency," Captain William F. Sheeley, a flight surgeon, warned the Eighth Air Force early in the war. "Many men seen in the hospital will not return to duty for months—if ever."

The men were often no better off on the ground; standard medical practice was to wait for "everything to drop off that is going to drop off," and treat what remained, often by amputating hands, feet, ears, and noses.

The Eighth's "aero-medical nightmare," as one historian called it, also included oxygen deprivation (anoxia), experienced to some degree by about half of the airmen, and chronic inflammation of the middle ear (aerotitis media) due to high altitude flights in non-pressurized cabins, which was responsible for two-thirds of the cases that temporarily grounded fliers. The Air Force had spent years debating bombing strategy but had given little thought to protecting its airmen at high altitudes.

They responded by blaming the airmen. As the Air Force's journal reported in October 1943,

> One waist gunner tried to change his oxygen mask at high altitude and took the easier way, removing his electrically heated glove. In a few seconds his right hand was frozen so badly he was unable to use it again—and his formation was under attack by Fw 190s. Other gunners have suffered severe frostbite because they forgot, after replacing their gloves, to plug them again into the suit's electric system.

They would spend the rest of the war trying to catch up, trying to reduce frostbite causalities.

My father's frostbite, three weeks shy of his twentieth birthday, would bother him for the rest of his life. It was on his bad left hand. Into his nineties, he was seeing doctors to have parts cut off. When I'd ask him why he was seeing a doctor for his hand, he said only, "It's nothing. An inconvenience."

## MAINZ AND ULM

The day after he froze two fingers, he was in the air again, flying to another railroad marshaling yard, this one in Mainz, Germany. They were back in *Heavenly Body*, which had put them in jeopardy with engine trouble two weeks earlier, and they were carrying a different kind of bomb—twenty, 260-pound fragmentation bombs. They were usually used to pierce armored vehicles. The flak was "intense," he wrote. "Lost No. 2 [engine], Nose Gunner wounded, Nose turret dome shattered, about 15 flak holes." Forty percent of the 1,140 bombers sent to Western Germany that day were damaged. Seven airmen were killed, 150 were missing and thirteen were wounded.

Under moderate cloud cover, 265 B-24s bombed Mainz guided by radar. "Results—Bombs dropped all over town," he wrote. The intelligence report concurred, mapping a trail of high explosive "bursts . . . dispersed over a large region"—in the city center, in "lightly built-up areas" and fields four, five, and six miles to the east and southeast, and in more fields two miles south and two miles east. All over town and beyond.

His third mission in as many days took him to an ordinance depot in Ulm, Germany. They were flying *Curly*, which was on its first mission since it was shot up over the Zuider Zee and came close to exploding.

Ulm was overcast—"10/10ths" clouds. For results my father wrote only a question mark. The confidential interpretation of the reconnaissance photos taken after the bombing said that the "most important" depot buildings were "razed by fire."

Under "Comments" he wrote "B-24 goes down in flames. One chute." One man missing in action. Nine men killed.

## DEBRIEFING

He refused to talk about the war, but late in life he was writing stories. At first he'd sit in the bagel bakery writing longhand. He was a regular. The guys there asked him what he was up to.

The stories he sent me were like old Hollywood romances of the 1930s and 1940s: Boy meets gal. She's swell. They dance. But there's another guy. Much dialogue ensues on the way to a happy ending.

In some stories, his leading man was Harry, an inventor, or other times an artist with a horse named Sam he'd take up to the mountains on his painting trips. And always there were "beautiful women." As he said, "If Mark Twain were alive, he'd have nothing to fear from me." But he enjoyed writing his stories. As he lost his eyesight, he switched to speaking his stories into the tape recorder we sent him.

But in one story, in his last year, the past came calling, literally, with a knock at the door. And there was his girlfriend, Judith, from England when he had just turned twenty. Judith was his first serious girlfriend. In the story this English woman has come to Long Island to a see a lawyer, my brother, as it happens. She's only in her late forties, and my father, or whoever he is in the story—his remembered self and the story character all intermixed—is also in his late forties, and conveniently divorced.

He doesn't recognize her at first. She has to prompt him: "Do you remember me?" She does look familiar and there's that English accent. "You don't remember me?" She repeats her name and he thinks to himself, "who the hell is this—wait a minute." He's surprised; he can't believe that she's shown up on his front steps. "The years haven't touched you," he says more than once. She still has her beautiful English accent.

He'd met her at a dance run by the synagogue near Old Buckenham, in the small city of Norwich, home to a Jewish community going back to the Middle Ages. "She was a little thing, five foot two or three. She spoke Yiddish with this cultured English accent," he said. As they danced, they'd sing with the band. "She had a beautiful voice." He was smitten.

In the story, he invites her in for coffee. She's bought him muffins, a staple of his late years. They talk: "Are you happy?" he asks her—that sort of thing. The imaginary visit leads him to recall a deep memory. It's a kind of self-therapy.

*So, we were back from a bombing mission. All crew members were ushered into intelligence. Debriefing. What'd you see? What you didn't see? And they would do something with the information. God only knows what. Also, we were given a shot of Scotch whiskey, which is what the Air Force did—figured you were a little jittery. There was an understatement. I always gave mine to one of the other crew members because I didn't like whiskey.*

But after a few missions, he welcomed the drink. "Every time I went, I would accept the mission-free whiskey."

After a mission, Judith was often waiting for him. Once he'd been debriefed, and had his shot of whiskey, she met him with a "hug and a kiss." "Most of the time I came back so knocked out, so tired I couldn't move." But, he said, "I liked nothing better than spending the aftershock with her."

She was "glad to see me still in one piece. Well, a few times I was lucky. And a few times my buddies were not."

He had returned from a rough mission, a long one, seven hours in the air, four hours on oxygen, a "Maximum Effort," when the Eighth Air Force dispatched most of the heavy bombers it had, sending a thousand or more sometimes as deep into Germany as Berlin.

*The things I saw on the way there and back were best forgotten. Particularly one incident where we passed a squadron of B-17s. One of them blew up. Literally, just exploded. Got hit with anti-aircraft fire. That was the end of nine or ten guys. The aircraft just blew up and we didn't see any parachutes. And that left an impression on me. I was wondering, when is this going to happen to me—or if.*

He didn't note the loss of this B-17 in his mission log. Nor did he record watching a B-24 go down into the Channel or the North Sea.

*On another mission we were coming back and off our right wing was another Liberator and he was obviously in trouble. He was sagging, and you could see it was faltering and we watched him go into the water. They landed on the water. I never found out what happened to them, but the Liberator had a penchant for breaking in half when it hit the water. But then I saw it was still in one piece. And I was grateful for that.*

There's no telling what else he saw out beyond his machine gun, but as he said, "I saw too many things I didn't want to see. It took the starch out of me."

"When I first saw you when I came back, I was so glad to see you, it almost brought tears to my eyes," he said, addressing the imaginary visitor in his story. "And you invited me up to your place, took me up to your apartment. We sat down and I had another shot. I was still a little jittery. You put your arms around me with a big, heavy hug, a smile, and a kiss. And I said, let me just rest awhile and we'll sit and talk."

"I sat down and I could see your bedroom." He asked her,

*"Do you mind if I lie down a little while?" And I lie down and you took my shoes off. Gave me another shot of whiskey and helped me to calm down the jitters from the last bombing mission. And you gave me a big, fat kiss, put the covers over me, and then proceeded to help me off with my trousers. You hung them up.*

*I stretched out and you gave me another big kiss and a hug. And I went to sleep. I could never hold my liquor. I went to sleep and after a while, you came in, got partially disrobed and crawled in behind me, put your arms around me, and held me real tight. That felt good.*

*And the jitters slowly disappeared. And that was one of the better days.*

And that's it. Not a pause, a wink, a suggestion that anything more happened. The commanding officers at the time talked of their bomber crews as men sometimes and as boys at other times. They were a mix; my "boy-men" one major called them. And here a boy-man, nearly twenty, was relieved to be held after a terrifying mission. Maybe she was his first; there's no way to know.

"There's nothing like it, I'm sure, like falling asleep in the arms of a beautiful woman," he said.

He woke up a long time later, having slept through half of a three-day pass. He didn't know what day it was. He got up and went into the kitchen. "I saw my uniform hanging there, all pressed. My cap was dusted off. And there was water boiling. She was making tea. I felt almost perfect, like a new man." They spent his remaining time on the pass together.

The visit with the past continued. They talk over old times, this old man of ninety-four, who's nearing fifty in the story, recalling himself at twenty. "Was I in love with you? I don't know. I was twenty years old, what do I know about love?"

On his twentieth birthday, September 28, 1944, he was between missions. Three days before he had flown to bomb Koblenz. In two days he'd fly to bomb the railroad yards at Hamm. In nine days, over Kassel, he'd be hit by shrapnel and would be carried off the plane in a stretcher, earning his first Purple Heart.

Later in the story, he resumes his character of a late forty-year-old divorcee who didn't have anyone in his life. "I've had a chance or two. . . . I thought I was in love, but nothing compared to 1944." So maybe he did love Judith. She wanted to marry him. After he was wounded, he was sent back to the states. She wrote to him. He never answered.

## It's a Wonderful Life

The psychological terrors of the bomber crews were thrice buried. The airmen hid any signs of mental breakdown and their commanding officers did their best not to report them. A few cases made their way to the Air Force psychiatrists at the newly created First Central Medical Establishment. Those men, after being examined, mostly ended up back in the bombers. The psychiatrists' job was to keep the fliers in the air. Of the 225,000 men who flew combat missions in the Eighth Air Force, only four to five thousand were officially reported as "emotional causalities." And of those only 2,100 were permanently grounded. And yet almost every flier who completed a tour of duty suffered one or more symptoms of a nervous or physical breakdown broadly called "combat fatigue." The British medical establishment's diagnosis had a sharper edge—"psychoneurosis."

The psychiatrists reviewed cases of "fear of flying," "apprehension," "jittery and depressed" men, and men who were "scared to death." They wrote down their family histories, alert to any signs of family instability, noting "somewhat nervous" mothers and "excitable" sisters, reviewed their combat records, and then often prescribed a sedative (sodium amytal) followed by a week at a rest home and a return to "full flying duties." If they grounded everyone who was "scared to death," few would be flying.

The psychology of the era was a blunt tool. Psychologists were trying to define "normal" in a time that was not normal—In what way was it sensible to fly to your own possible death day after day? The normal, healthy organism heads in the opposite direction. He outruns the lion and leaps the river; he stays in his burrow until the predator has left. He doesn't turn around and dance past the lion day after day.

The flight surgeons, psychiatrists, and psychologists could not settle on what to call the upset and turmoil they were seeing in the bomber crews. Was it a "severe aero-anxiety state" or "flying fatigue" or "war weariness"? They said, variously, that it was due to severe homesickness, or "the breakdown of the ego's defense against anxiety" brought on by combat. They unspooled a long list of distress: anxiety dreams, insomnia, depression, seclusiveness, anorexia, agitation, tremors, dizziness, blurring vision, inability to concentrate, binge drinking, and a loss of confidence.

They tried to chart it. For the first ten missions, a bomber crewman was anxious, then in the next ten he settled in, but his anxiety returned with his last ten missions. Even if the mission was a "milk run," it now seemed more dangerous. "After seventeen or eighteen raids you get to worrying more and more because one shell will do it," said an airman. "At first, you're glad when you have an easy target, but toward the end, even a raid over France no longer looks easy. You figure one shell will be enough. Toward the end you get more tense on every raid. On the last raid I was most tense of all."

This, the psychiatrists decided, was a normal "fear reaction"—what the airmen jokingly called "Focke-Wulf Jitters" or being "Flak Happy"—but fear could linger and cripple the airmen. They knew how the war had ended for many of their buddies and could imagine their own fate. "They see the wing on fire, or their blood spattered over the cockpit window, or their crew freezing in a dinghy in the North Sea or drifting down in a parachute into a German field," wrote one psychiatrist. Imagination, it was said, could be a soldier's worst enemy.

"Combat left its mark upon most returning gunners. Ninety percent of the men experienced fear in combat equal to or more severe than any other fear they had ever experienced," said a report by Air Force psychologists. A study of five thousand gunners who had returned from fighting found that 20 percent had been wounded in aerial combat, 42 percent were in a plane that had crash landed or ditched in the water, and eight percent had been forced to bail out. Twenty percent had been on missions where one or more of their fellow crewmen had been wounded or killed. "The typical returned gunner reported that approximately half of his close friends were killed, missing, or wounded in combat."

Approximately 45 percent of the gunners they studied "had suffered from some form of personality disorder as a result of their combat experiences." They did not miss combat—81.4 percent did not plan to volunteer for a second tour of duty. (Only nine percent "liked the excitement of combat gunnery.")

Back home in the states, the war clung to them. The psychologists questioned 2,659 gunners who had returned from combat in 1944. More than half of the returnees said that "since returning from overseas duty" they were sometimes "easily confused or 'rattled,'" were "now bothered with sleepless nights," sometimes had "shaking or trembling hands or knees or muscular twitches," and sometimes found it "difficult to concentrate on tasks" and make decisions. Close to half reported they sometimes had nightmares, were "now restless or not able to sit still," were "easily exhausted or all tired out," sometimes "felt sick" to the "stomach" or "felt that" they "could vomit." "Loud and sudden sounds" sometimes made them "jumpy." And sometimes they had "fears" that drove them out of their minds. Close to 85 percent said they sometimes or often felt "'blue' or depressed." Only 15.2 percent said they were never depressed.

Home at last, the veterans were sometimes depressed, sleepless, jumpy, restless, indecisive, confused, and overcome with fear. Their answers to the survey punch the ticket for Post-Traumatic Stress Disorder (PTSD) long before that term was used, but the wartime psychologists never spoke of trauma. They said that most of the gunners were showing signs of a "moderate degree of combat fatigue" or a "psychiatric disorder." If they thought the airmen were more damaged than this, their military duties seem to have precluded worse conclusions. There are hints of darker days in their reports, such as noting that some returning gunners now doubted "the reason for and the necessity of fighting the war."

They wanted to find out how a "normal" male could be expected to behave in the Air War. Could they create a psychological profile that would reveal who would break down under fire? Or would every man break down? But there was nothing normal about the commuter war, about fighting a war that was distant and also close-in, sudden and immediate.

Each tour of duty recorded in the Army's "201" file had its own, unrecorded shadow file.

Seven days after winning an academy award for *The Philadelphia Story* in March 1941, Jimmy Stewart enlisted, months before the country was at war. He had been turned down on his first attempt because he was ten pounds underweight. One of the most famous movie stars in America was now a buck private in the Army, his monthly salary reduced from $6,000 to $21. Stewart really wanted to fly. He had logged more than three-hundred hours as a private pilot and had his own airplane, but he was close to thirty-three years old, far older than the aviation cadets in their twenties who were becoming pilots. The Army treated him as a celebrity and refused to send him to fight. Stewart transferred to the Air Force and began a two-and-a-half-year-long campaign to be shipped overseas. While he waited, he qualified to fly twin-engine and four-engine aircraft, trained other pilots to fly the B-17, and kept logging flying time. When others were assigned to bomber crews and sent overseas, he was held back, denied his chance to fly in combat. The Army classified him as "static personnel," limited to stateside service. They didn't want to lose a movie star.

He finally made it to England in November 1943 as a squadron leader in the newly formed 445th BG. He flew a dozen missions as a B-24 pilot and was officially commended for his good judgment under fire. He had good rapport with his men. He inspired confidence; they believed in him, and thus in each other. He flew often and did not cherry-pick the easier missions, saying, "I just can't sit here and send these fellows to death, without knowing myself what I am sending them into." They said Jimmy Stewart was a "lucky squadron leader." Everyone wanted to be favored by good luck.

Major Stewart was promoted to Group Operations Officer and sent down the road nine miles to the 453rd at Old Buckenham, where Ramsey Potts was just beginning to put the group in good working order. "The Group Operations Officer runs the war," said Gen. Andrew Low, who was Stewart's assistant, and later replaced him. "He runs the missions each day." He decides which planes and bombs they need for each mission. "Potts and Stewart hit it off from the start," says Starr Smith, an intelligence officer who served with them. "Individually, they were natural born leaders; together, they were a formidable team."

When the airmen at the 453rd were told they were getting a movie star, they were not impressed. They thought it might be a publicity stunt, a star turn for an actor to fly a few missions and play at war, before being shipped home pronto. But Stewart wasn't just another movie star passing through. He was serious, working through the night planning the missions of the 453rd, staying in the tower until the last crew had returned. He flew tough missions with them—more than the commanding officers wanted—and was said to wipe missions he flew off the board so he wouldn't reach his limit. My father had the greatest respect for Stewart. He did his own flying, he said. He was a real pilot.

Few men really knew him, though they saw him in the mess for breakfast before missions and he would show up at the officers' club, sometimes playing the piano and singing one of his favorites, *Ragtime Cowboy Joe*. He's there in a few posed photos. Walking with others toward the camera he looks tall, rangy, and smart in his uniform, Hollywood handsome, more an airman than the others. In another photo with four others studying maps, he forgets the camera and is lost in his work. He blends right in. You have to search to pick him out. That's how he wanted it.

Stewart refused all publicity. He turned away the Air Force public relations staff who wanted stories. His base was off limits to the press until they convinced him he was denying his men the chance to be in their hometown newspapers. After that the press was allowed in, but only to write about the men of the 453rd.

He was a "superb briefer," said Starr Smith. Like any good actor, he rehearsed. Young actor Sgt. Walter Matthau (then spelled Matthow) used to sneak into the briefings just to see Jimmy Stewart "do his Jimmy Stewart." At first the men were a little star struck, but he made them forget all that and see that "he was one of the boys. He was marvelous to watch," said Matthau. Stewart concluded his briefings, saying, "Well, fellas. This is it. I—uh—I want you all back here safe. That understood? Fine."

The war aged Jimmy Stewart. He suffered terribly when his men didn't return from a mission. He couldn't sleep. "I was really afraid of what the dawn might bring. Our group had suffered several casualties during the day, and the next morning at dawn I was going to have to lead my squadron out again, deep into Germany," he said when he was a squadron leader. "I got to imagining what might happen, and I feared the worst. Fear is an insidious and deadly thing. It can warp judgment, freeze reflexes, breed mistakes. And worse, it's contagious. I felt my own fear and knew that if it wasn't checked, it could infect my crew members."

He returned to church for the first time in years and reread the 91st psalm, which his father had put in his parting letter to his son: *I will say of the Lord, He is my refuge and my fortress: my God; in him will I trust.*

"I tried with all my might to lead and protect them," he said of the airmen of the 445th and the 453rd.

*I lost a few men—all my efforts, all my prayers couldn't stand between them and their fates, and I grieved over them, blamed myself, even. But my father said something wonderful to me when I came home after the war. He said, "Shed all blame, shed all guilt, Jim. You know you did your very best, and God and Fate, both of which are beyond any human being's efforts, took care of the rest."*

He "had come near to the point of complete exhaustion," says a credible wartime magazine story written by a fellow bomber pilot. "Combat fatigue" was so common it was usually left unsaid. Lieutenant Jon Schueler, a navigator in the 303rd BG, said, "I started to feel guilty, responsible for every death. I was not sleeping, afraid that I'd make errors and cause the death of many. It could happen—navigation errors, pilot errors. Ending in death. Planes falling, planes shot down. So many were dying and I felt responsible." He lost twenty pounds and was "skinny as a rail." The flight surgeon gave him sleeping pills and took him out of combat. He worked planning the missions. But he was still in the fight. "At the end of the day I was on the tower, looking to the sky, watching for the returning planes, counting when they appeared. One, two, three, four . . . nine, ten, eleven, twelve . . . twelve . . . twelve . . . there are no others." One was missing; the rest were "badly shot up," landing with wounded aboard.

Schueler was moved up to headquarters, but the comfort of his private room, "superb food," and the entire atmosphere felt like a staged play cut off from "the reality of flight and fear and death . . . comradeship and effort and being alive. . . . I felt dead amongst the living. I felt weak, washed out, through." Schueler collapsed from illness and depression. He was hospitalized and, in time, given an honorable discharge.

Stewart came home a changed man. His parents were upset by how much he had aged. He was thinner; his face looked tighter. He was losing his hair and it was graying. He had also lost some hearing. The press asked him about his gray hair. He said: "It got pretty rough overseas at times." A friend who hadn't seen him in two years ran into him on the troopship home and noted how he had changed. "He was more nervous and a little bit shaky." Stewart told a hometown friend that he was so upset during the war he had trouble eating. Soft foods like peanut butter and ice cream were all he could eat. He had no appetite. He reportedly had nightmares and would for years.

He moved in with his good friend, Henry Fonda, who was home after three years in the Navy. They sat quietly, intensely, building model airplanes out of balsa. They also flew kites. Stewart didn't make a movie for a year. Other, younger-looking stars were now playing the roles he used to get. He refused to glamorize his war service, refused to make a film: *The Jimmy Stewart Story*. "I saw too much suffering. It's certainly not something to talk about—or celebrate. Sherman said, 'War is Hell'—how right he was, how truly he spoke." He never talked about what he had been through. He wasn't going to tell any war stories.

"My father's experiences during World War II affected him more deeply and permanently than anything else in his life. Yet his children grew up knowing almost nothing about those years," said his daughter Kelly Stewart Harcourt. "Dad never talked about the war. My siblings and I knew only that he had been a pilot, and that he had won some medals, but that he didn't see himself as a hero."

*It's a Wonderful Life* was the first movie he made after the war and his anger in that film is raw, edgy, and seems to break the confines of the sentimental story. In a famous scene, praying for help—"I'm not a praying man but if you're up there and you can hear me, show me the way. I'm at the end of my rope. Show me the way, God"—he's overcome, crying in an unscripted moment, surprising the director. "As I said those words," Stewart said later, "I felt the loneliness, the hopelessness of people who had nowhere to turn, and my eyes filled with tears. I broke down sobbing. That was not planned at all." His anger and upset also surprised audiences who were used to a gentler man. They didn't like the movie and the studio lost money. *It's a Wonderful Life* failed at the box office. That anger was Stewart's PTSD and it showed on the set, according to one biographer. But that is an overreach. There are no medical records to check, and he was reticent to the point of disappearing. Like many who served, he came home older and exhausted, but he kept his sorrows and remorse to himself. He, too, hid the psychological terrors of the war.

When a plane was coming apart, the men who had to jump and had survived, said that once they were clear of the bomber and the chute opened, they were enveloped by the quiet. They'd leapt from fiery explosions and men dying into a quiet sky. In moments, they'd hit the ground or a tree. They might break a leg, be taken prisoner, be hanged from a lamppost, or hidden by the resistance. They might be killed hitting the ground. But those moments when they had fallen clear of the crashing plane were quiet—they were a reprieve. In those few moments, they belonged to the sky, not the war.

## "When Censorship Ceases"

His notes from the September 10, 1944, mission to Ulm are the last ones I have. Ulm was his thirteenth mission, and since two were recalled, this left him only about a third of the way to completing his tour. His notes were seized by the base censor who inserted this typed notice:

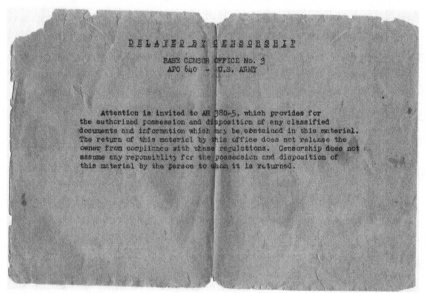

Delayed by censorship.

Airmen were forbidden to keep dairies. Their notes could be found if they were shot down. Each side was eager for any information about their enemy. Captured airmen would later talk about how they were interrogated before being sent to a POW camp. "How's your brother Morton and your sister Irma? Did they also go to school at PS 56 like you did?" Things like that. It was unnerving. The German intelligence apparatus carefully read American newspapers and magazines. But my father, like the many others who kept hidden diaries, was only doing what the Air Force's many intelligence officers were working long hours to do: trying to make sense of this war, trying to get Mission #554 and the hundreds of other missions to tell a story that would have an old-fashioned beginning, middle, and an end with victory, parades, and peace.

I don't know how his brief mission diary was discovered, but oddly he had totaled up his flying time on the last page as if he were getting ready to be shipped out to another assignment, possibly on the ground. He wrote: "Training and non-operational time 115 hrs (app.) Combat time"—and here he added up each mission to get "81:35 hrs." He also totaled the bombs. He had taken part in dropping more than thirty-seven tons of high explosives on France and Germany.

His "Private Diary or Memoranda" was "placed in storage" to be "forwarded as directed when censorship ceases." After the war, the Army Air Forces mailed his diary back to 1639 Monroe Ave. in the Bronx, just as they had promised.

## WEISSENHORN

Three days after he had seen a B-24 go down in flames, he saw another shot down, this one nearby, in his formation. Their mission was to destroy a Luftwaffe fuel depot in Weissenhorn, Germany. They were crossing the Rhine, about one hundred miles northwest of the depot, when an uncharted flak battery fired, hitting two bombers.

My father, flying again in *Curly*, saw one hit up close, a few hundred feet out his gun port.

*There's one of our comrades flying another Liberator off our left wing and all of a sudden he started to sputter. We didn't see any anti-air-craft fire, but all of a sudden white smoke began to pour from his air-plane. That was a Capt. Mills. All of a sudden men started jumping out of the airplane, parachuting. I counted seven parachutes. And they went down and that was that. That was the end of them,*

He said that on a tape that he had recorded but never sent. We found the tape three years after he died.

Pilot Eugene Mills in *Porky* was flying at the center of their formation.

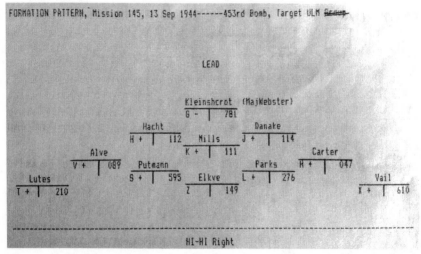

The formation for the mission to Ulm.

Captain Eino Alve, who had brought *Curly* home on two engines three weeks earlier, was flying *Star Eyes* close to Mills. "A B-24 flying above and to our right received a direct hit. Fragments from the same shell struck our plane, causing a flat tire," wrote Alve. "I could see the cockpit of his plane burning. I saw him struggling in the flames. There I sat, powerless to save his life. Then his plane veered over us, nearly taking us with him. We saw one chute open, but officially everyone was listed as missing in action. Depression settled in thick and heavy that night when we saw the empty bunks."

My father counted seven chutes; Alve saw one. With everything in motion, it was like each man could only see a few frames of a movie. The reports say three crewmen survived.

The other bomber that was hit managed to fly about three hundred miles toward home before crash-landing near Belgium, in Prouvy, France.

The Weissenhorn mission received poor marks. The 453rd, with forty-five bombers, was alone in bombing the camouflaged fuel storage depot "situated in a large woods." "The storage tanks are apparently undamaged," said an intelligence report. They did destroy "a small group of industrial buildings" and the camouflage netting.

The execution of the mission was criticized in the "tactical analysis" at division headquarters. The 2nd Combat Wing, which included the 453rd, flew "erratically on route" and "withdrew erratically." For much of the way there they "flew south of briefed route, ten to twenty miles" and "withdrew north of the briefed route five to fifteen miles." The entire 2nd Air Division was "sprawled out," said another assessment, due to "high cloud and dense persistent contrails which seriously handicapped their flying. As a result, one combat wing abandoned the mission entirely, as did some squadrons of other wings who lost their parent groups in the soup." The ordinance depot in Ulm, to which 135 bombers were dispatched, wasn't attacked. At the fuel depot, the lead bombardier in the second squadron of the 453rd "had trouble identifying the target."

## KOBLENZ, HAMM, AND LACHEN-SPEYERDORF

Bad weather grounded the bombers for a week, giving their crews a reprieve. After flying practice formations, Vail and his crew, with sixty-six other bombers, returned to Germany to bomb a railroad yard in Koblenz in solid overcast. Neighborhoods a half mile to the east and more than a mile to the southwest were also hit.

A few days later, on September 25, the first bomber my father had flown in combat, the *Mary Harriet*, with a different crew, was in a midair collision with a B-17. The *Mary Harriet's* formation had dropped its bombs and was rallying for its return home when they became entangled with a formation of B-17s headed to the target. Six feet of the *Mary Harriet's* left wing was torn off. The bomber made it back to an RAF airfield a few miles from the Channel. "Pilot was not responsible for accident," the aircraft accident officer ruled. The pilot "flying in very close formation at the time was unable to take any action to avoid the collision. Accident responsibilities lies 100% with squadron of B-17s, (identification unknown)."

Hamm, one of the largest railroad yards in Germany, was next. It was a gateway to the industries in the Ruhr Valley. They bombed Hamm twice in four days. In the first attack, on September 30, more than two hundred B-24s dropped bombs in heavy overcast. The results were "unobserved." Twelve aircraft from the 453rd, "separated from the formation due to contrails," misjudged the flares marking another attack thirty miles away and bombed Munster by mistake, as did another bomber group. On the following mission, with a third more bombers, Hamm was judged to be "well hit." A day later, the intelligence report said that "many fires are still raging in this town."

This mission, too, was criticized for ragged flying. "Bomber formation very poor, CW's [Combat Wings] not in briefed order, weaved and overran each other. Several units twenty miles apart making escort difficult," said a confidential report from the headquarters of Eighth Fighter Command.

On that second mission to Hamm, October 2, the 453rd lost *Shack Happy*. The pilot, Lt. James A. Emerson, age 29, had completed his tour and had also been awarded the Distinguished Flying Cross. He was a newlywed. Once his British wife had the papers she needed, he would return with her to his hometown in Iowa. While he waited for the necessary documents, Emerson volunteered to fly a few more missions. Hamm was his thirty-ninth, and last, mission.

*Shack Happy* arrived at the target late, and was hit from above by a bomb dropped from a plane in the 389th BG. The bomb didn't go off, but broke the plane in two, setting it on fire. *Shack Happy*, in a "sheet of flames," plummeted to earth. There were no survivors.

The next day they bombed a Luftwaffe airfield in Lachen-Speyerdorf, Germany. The Luftwaffe had been pushed out of airfields in France and Belgium. The Eighth Air Force was pursing them in Germany. They wanted to destroy as many of their airplanes as possible on the ground. Flying through flak that was "heavy, intense, inaccurate," more than one hundred B-24s bombed the airfield, hitting about twenty-five hangars, huts, and other buildings around the grass field. "Very good results," said the intelligence assessment. "GPs [General Purpose bombs] seen to burst squarely on the main installations at the eastern end of the airfield in numerous good patterns and hits seen on most of main installations, perimeter and landing ground. . . damage to this target probably severe."

## KASSEL

In the "greatest coordinated aerial assault of the war" to that date, said the press release from the United States Strategic Air Force in Europe, more than fourteen hundred bombers and nine hundred fighters were sent to synthetic oil plants, armament, tank, and airplane factories, as well as thirty-five other targets. It was a "Maximum Effort."

The Luftwaffe rose to meet "one of the strongest heavy bomber forces ever" with its latest strategy: forty to fifty fighters swarmed the lead bombers. "They made a mass attack from the rear high to level in waves of eight to ten abreast peeling off to right, left, and some going under formation," said a mission report. "Pilots were very aggressive." The "attack lasted for approximately eight minutes, and although supporting fighters were in the immediate area and attacked . . . they were unable to prevent a loss of twelve B-17s." The bombers litter the mission reports: "Two B-17s were seen to explode in air and one spun down. . . . Two B-17s seen to crash in woods. . . . Two chutes seen from one . . . six B-17s exploded over target, 29,000 feet, no chutes seen."

It was a day of hard-fought battles. The Germans defended reservoirs with barrage balloons. They created a smoke screen at the Politz oil refinery, fired at the bombers with "intense, heavy, and accurate" flak, launched seventeen V-1 flying bombs toward London (five hit), and deployed an "exceptional number of jet and rocket propelled" aircraft.

Jets and rocket planes were a new threat. The first ones had only been seen a few months earlier—"Buck Rogers flashes" making "a wild and breathless pass," said the Eighth Air Force's newsletter, *Target Victory*. They were the subject of fascinating reports and descriptions that sound like the UFO reports to come after the war. Sketches and descriptions were sent to headquarters. "The e/a [enemy aircraft] was described as very maneuverable, weaving until opening fire. Its radius of turn seemed very short while gliding, and the attacks were aggressive and pressed home in each instance," says a tactical analysis report.

They had encountered the breakthrough Me 163 Komet, a stubby, bat-winged rocket-powered plane. "The Me 163 seemed more triangular in appearance than shown in conventional silhouette. . . . The maximum speed of the Me 163 was judged to be about 400 mph and they did not seem faster than P-51s. All smoke emitted . . . was very white in appearance and appeared as a streak or round column of vapor." Actually, the rocket plane could reach speeds over 600 mph, so fast it whizzed by the bombers, giving the pilot only 2.5 seconds to get a shot off, and it burned through its fuel in just seven minutes, having to glide home, which is when the suddenly obsolescent propeller-driven fighters would shoot them down. That day, October 7, fighters shot down four jets and another eighteen airplanes. "The jet pilots appeared to be trainees," they reported. Eleven of the Air Force's fighters were lost. The fighters also chased off a P-51 Mustang over the Zuider Zee erroneously believed to have been captured, strafed many planes and trains on the ground, and one fighter group reported: "German heard on our frequency."

The Eighth Air Force's losses were steep. Forty bombers were shot down and half of all the bombers flying that day were damaged, almost all from the usual flak and fighters. Eight shot-up bombers landed in Switzerland, where their crews would be held until the war's end. Another ditched at sea, and one crash-landed back in England. Six men were killed in action, thirty-nine were wounded, and 367 were missing.

The 453rd's small corner of the days' activities was the Henschel Tiger tank factory and the Henschel Aero Engine Works at Kassel, one of the top targets for the Eighth Air Force (number six on the list). They repeatedly bombed the factories. After the raids of October 2 and 7, the

Nazi's minister of war production, Albert Speer, conceded that Henschel was destroyed.

Over Kassel, on October 7, my father was hit by flak. He was flying his nineteenth mission. The average number of missions that crew members lived to complete was fifteen. He'd beaten one average, but the average life of a bomber crew in Europe from August 1944 through January 1945 was 115 combat days. He had flown sixty-eight days in combat. In civilian life, two months could go by in a haze of habit and routine, days that were forgotten as they were lived. But war days were different; they could plant themselves in memory and never leave.

When I was younger I asked him about where he was wounded. "The back of the legs and the buttocks," he said after hesitating. But it was worse than that. In one of his taped stories he mentions that he had grown a mustache after he got home. "What's that mustache you have?" he was asked. "It's just to cover up a shaving scar," he says. "This was a lie, of course. It was from some flak that got me in the face. The rest of the wounds were taken care of."

In the air, he'd have to lie there wounded for many hours. If he was fortunate, someone in his crew would put powdered sulfa and bandages on his wounds and give him a shot of morphine. That would have been first-class medical care.

On a day when 1,400 bombers were dropping 3,188 tons of explosives and the Germans were firing tons of steel and explosives skyward, an ounce or two of steel hit a twenty-year-old Bronx boy. It's just ounces and inches. An inch more one way and it's a near miss, a story to be told over a pint or two at the pub, an inch or two another way, and it could mean death, his family sitting shiva for him. But he was alive and flying home to Old Buc with a good pilot.

## G. I. PARADISE

After he was wounded, he passed through a series of hospitals and was sent back to the states. He would be hospitalized for 164 days. He crossed the ocean again, less gloriously this time, on a troopship, ending up at the

Army hospital at Mitchel Field on Long Island. Once the worst of his flak wounds and frostbite were healing, he was sent to a rehabilitation hospital on the idyllic, forested seven-hundred-acre campus of a former prep school in Pawling, New York. The press called it a "G.I. Paradise." My father agreed. "My time spent there was a sinecure. It was a good deal—it was like a country club." There were golf links, tennis courts, an indoor pool, a gym, bridle paths, trout streams, skiing nearby, and, said *Life* magazine, "a full bucolic roster of cows, chickens, pigs, barns, farmland, and gardens."

The Army Air Force Convalescent Center in Pawling was a new experiment. It was the first convalescent center not on an Army base. Military rules were relaxed. Each man was told that "Pawling exists only for his benefit and welfare." With a doctor, each man worked out a daily, six-hour schedule of therapy, exercise, classes, and farm work, depending on what he needed. The hospital welcomed visitors and encouraged the men to go home on weekends. It was also the first hospital in the country to pioneer using therapy dogs to help depressed soldiers. They had a kennel of therapy dogs. More than 90 percent of Pawling's patients returned to duty.

"In this rehabilitation hospital there were two classes of patients; surgical, which was on my floor, and the people with emotional problems, or as we called them cruelly, Jungle Jolly. They were on the third floor," my father said.

> *The program there was for all the patients to relax and get back into the real-life routine, which we all did. They had us going to classes, just like in school. They had a class in the human body, a class in government, a class in blind flying, which I needed like another hole in my head. And we also had other activities. Every Saturday night there was a dance, and the girls would come from Vassar, a fancy girls' school. We would size them up and dance with them. We really had only two things on our minds. And it was girls and getting out of the Army and girls.*

There were movies, dances, or stage shows every night.

*We had people coming from the USO to entertain us. I remember an old Vaudevillian by the name of Benny Fields would come over and sing a few songs for us. And then one day the piano played an introduction, and a big Black guy came out in sailor suit, a kid's sailor suit, on a peg leg. His name was Peg Leg Bates. And he did a dance to music on that peg leg that was positively enthralling. We had a few amputees there at the hospital and I'm sure he was brought there for them to see what you can do if you have to. I remember Peg Leg Bates, a smile on his face, a great sense of humor. And what a dancer, even with his peg leg.*

At least one hour of physical activity daily was required. "We went tobogganing there. We went skiing where Lowell Thomas had a property nearby." There, on "Strawberry Hill," he met Lowell Thomas, the famous broadcaster who had made Lawrence of Arabia a household name. Thomas was still on the radio when I was in elementary school. I knew his voice coming from the radio on the little green table in the kitchen.

"Wow! What he'd say," my second-grade self asked.

"He called me by my first name."

"Really?"

"Yes. He said, 'Hello sergeant.'"

A kid-sized war story. So many follow-up questions this six-year-old reporter didn't ask—*What were you in the hospital for? Frostbite, you said? You had frostbite and they let you go skiing?*

They claimed that men had made great recoveries at Pawling. Col. Hobart H. Todd, a flight surgeon who had served in the South Pacific, was the hospital's commanding officer.

He would talk about a gunner who had lost a leg on a mission to bomb the Ploesti oil refineries. He spent several months in a hospital deeply depressed. "He came to us a thoroughly disheartened boy who couldn't use the prosthesis that had been given to him. Now he can run around the track faster than I can. He attends all the dances and even jitterbugs! If he walked in here now you couldn't tell he had an artificial limb. He is coming along marvelously and is a leader to other prosthetic cases."

They had nothing good to offer for my father's frostbite. Parts of his bad left hand had gotten gangrene and turned black. The Army doctors wanted to cut off a hefty portion of his left hand. He thought not. He'd just live with it. And he did—this injury was his life-long companion.

*The only mistake you made in that place was when the doctor came over and said, "How are you?" if you said, "I'm fine," they mark your papers "fit for duty" and they ship you out. And none of us wanted to leave there because it was such a good deal. It was so comfortable. So finally, one day I made the mistake of telling the doctor I was feeling fine, so he marked my papers "fit for duty" and they shipped me out.*

The look. Back home for a studio portrait on Madison Avenue.

Pawling, in the Hudson Valley, was a few hours by train and subway from the Bronx. My father returned home for the first time since he'd left for the war. "I was home on furlough, so my ma said to me, Go visit bubbe, your gandma. She's always asking for you." He went to see her.

*She ushered me into the house, gave me a big hug, and a big kiss on the cheek. Here she was my little grandma. She was about five feet tall and a refugee from Czarist Russia. And couldn't speak a word of English but understood everything you said. So she invited me in, hugged me again, and asked me in Yiddish, if I got hurt when I was in the Army—which I still was, I was still in uniform. And I told her, no I didn't get hurt, which was a lie. She said, "You didn't get hurt in the* milchamah*?" The Hebrew word for "war." I said, "No bubbe." Then she asked me, "Hast arafgelaz tbambes aoyf di deytshn? Did you drop bombs on the Germans?" "Yeah, bubbe. Yes, Grandma." "Gut, lomir esn," she said. "Good, let's eat."*

His bubbe had it right. War is killing. It's about destroying your neighbor, and this is what we avoid saying. *Did you kill Germans? Good. Let's eat.* It's compact. It's harsh. It's the truth.

He was sent to Army Air Forces Redistribution Station No. 1, the "replacement depot," at Atlantic City. The *Repple Depple*, G.I.s called it. At the start of the war, the Army had taken over forty-seven hotels, paying a dollar a room. They then packed them Army-style with bunk beds, four or five soldiers to a room, until the hotels were so overcrowded there was no water pressure in the evenings when everyone returned from the drill fields. The hotels were jammed. Even with constant, pre-announced fire drills, it was hard to evacuate the buildings. *The Saturday Evening Post* gave wartime Atlantic City the cozy name of Camp Boardwalk. "It was easy duty. Just report in and then go do what you want," he said.

He was free to go to dances. He dated a woman named Ann who would look into his eyes as they danced and say, "I can always tell when you're lying."

"How?"

"Your blue eyes turn gray."

"Oh, in that case I better watch myself."

Movie talk, right off the silver screen.

On the dance floor "younger and shorter men would try and cut in," he said. "She turned them all down, which made me feel good." They went to the beach together and swam in the ocean. He'd pick her up and throw her into the waves.

One day the Army called him in and said, "Tell us where you want to be shipped." The Army was really a vast shipping operation sending men by rail all over the country. He was still recuperating from his wounds. He'd heard there was a hospital on the Grand Concourse in the Bronx that was taking combat veterans. It was a five-minute walk from his parents. "Send me there," he said. "OK," the Army said. "We'll see what we can do." They shipped him to Georgia.

## "GREETINGS FROM SPENCE FIELD. KEEP 'EM FLYING"

Spence Field had been bulldozed out of 1,600 acres of swamp and tobacco fields just four years earlier. They had almost called its main street, Tobacco Road. A tall, red-and-white checkered water tower was the only thing that broke the flatness. It was "a little one-runway job where they were training French pilots," he said.

> *The climate in Moultrie, Georgia, on a hot day—which was Monday to Monday—the perspiration would pour off your back. That was my case. I wasn't used to it.*
>
> *I reported to the colonel, a man in about his sixties. He was getting ready to retire, a real gentleman. And he was glad to see me and we had a nice chat.*

A fan was cooling the colonel. Three women were working at desks, typing and filing papers. The colonel looked over his papers and asked about his civilian work as a draftsman. He thought he might have an assignment for him.

> *I was one of the few combat returnees at the airfield. And I looked with, well, disdain at some of them because I was such a cocky kid. I was wearing my beer ribbons—a ribbon for every medal or honor that you've won. It was mandatory. I was about twenty years old and*

*I had . . . my wings because I was an aerial gunner. I really savored it. Maybe a lot of people didn't like me because I was Jewish and I was also a combat returnee. But I didn't care because there were a lot of nice young ladies there. They always had a dance.*

He walked into the hangar.

*They had three AT-6s. North American built. Real rugged looking. There was a young lady standing on a platform working on an AT-6. She looked down at me and said, "Hey Pincus, hand me the torque wrench." This young lady was extremely attractive. She was also wearing her kid sister's coveralls. I handed her the torque wrench. I climbed up on the platform.*

*"Are you sure you know how to use this?" [That's a 1940s male speaking.]*

*"I'm an A & E," she said. An airframe and engine mechanic. You had to have a license for that, a civilian license, and she had it.*

And "she was a real good looking girl."

"I said, 'How'd you know my name was Pincus?' She said, 'There's no secrets at this secret Army base.'" Spence Field may have been one of the sleepiest corners of a world at war. Her name was Jane and what she knew of the world was her parcel of small-town Georgia.

"I'd say she was about 25 years old then. She took a shine to me. We'd go to lunch almost every day. She had a car there, not many people did. She had a 1936 DeSoto. What can I say about this car?" He stops the story to talk about her car. In other times a storyteller might pause to describe the landscape, the heather on the hills, the fog rolling in, but for my dad it was machines—cars, planes, radios. He never forgot an airplane, a car, a number of any sort, and, it seems, any woman who had been kind to him, going all the way back to Toby Kagan, the teen next door who looked after him when he was five years old.

The 1936 DeSoto was "the introduction to streamlining. Nice look-ing little machine. She tried, one time, to teach me to drive. I couldn't get the hang of that business with the clutch. She explained to me what it meant and all that. She really knew her stuff."

But the Desoto was about more than streamlining and learning to drive.

*Jane and I got to know each other, if you know what I mean. We used to get acquainted in the backseat of her car. And that got to be quite cramping, so one night we decided we were going to find a different place to be alone so we went to the baseball field and went to the dugout and we just stretched out there and we're going to get acquainted, as you see, and a light shined on us and a voice yelled out, "Sergeant, I'm coming back here in fifteen minutes. I don't want to find you here." So, I yelled out, "OK" and the two of us disappeared.*

He laughed. "Struck me funny. I got caught, in other words."

*As I said before, I was a pretty cocky kid. I thought I was the cat's meow as they say. So one day I go to call on Jane and her mother greets me at the door and says, "Jane can't go out with you today." And she's looking at me—her eyes look like they're boring a hole in my head. I say, "What's the matter?" She says, "She's sick." And then she looks at me and says, "She's not pregnant. Don't worry." That had never crossed my mind.*

But he thought, "Gee that could have happened, right?"

I don't know what he was doing for the war effort at Spence Field. I suppose he was boosting morale on the home front. He was, officially, clerking in the airfield office. This was, he said, "a great time in my life. No responsibility—except for that damn heat and humidity," and the strong Southern sun. Once again, he got a bad sunburn, so severe it hurt to move his arms and he had to report to sick call. But, as he said, "nobody was shooting at me and I didn't have to do any kitchen police or anything like that."

The grim truth was that he was waiting to be sent to the Pacific, even if he didn't care to recall that. In the spring and early summer of 1945, the Army was holding on to everyone, preparing for a possible November invasion of Japan that could kill millions of soldiers and civilians. But after Japan surrendered in August, his next stop would be home.

He was still in uniform, but casually. One day he had to bring some papers to a general across the field. In the heat, he had opened his shirt, rolled up his sleeves and had his cap way back on his head.

*I really didn't look very military. So, the general says, "Sergeant is that the way you dressed when you were in the Eighth Air Force?"*

*"No sir."*

*He proceeded to ream me out up and down. And all I kept saying was "Yes sir. No sir." He was telling me how I was out of uniform and this and that, which was all true. But it was so damn hot. I was perspiring; water was coming out of every pore of my body.*

The general, he could see, wore a shoulder patch from the Twelfth Air Force, which flew out of North Africa to open the Mediterranean to shipping and support the Allied invasions of Sicily and Italy. They'd both been in combat.

*So, he says, "What have you got to say for yourself sergeant?"*

*"No sir, no excuse, sir."*

*So he cracked a half smile, which he was trying to stifle, and he said, "Go on, get out of here."*

*So I saluted him. He half saluted me with half a smile and nothing ever came of it. I guess one combat returnee to another, we understood each other.*

The formalities of Army order were dismissed in the Georgia heat.

Army life held him loosely. "There was a dance coming up. And I found out that not only was Jane an A & E, but she also led the band at any dance that we gave. She sang beautifully." In addition to the dance band, the Spence Field Skylarks, the airfield also had a concert band and a drum and bugle corps to march the recruits around the drill field and add to the pomp and ceremony as they graduated a new class of aviation cadets every month.

*I went into the dance and there was Jane on the bandstand. She waved at me and I came over and said hello. And she asked me to sing a song. I said, "I'll try, I don't know how good I am." Turns out, that at that time in my life, I did have a good singing voice. And I did—I sang a duet with her. And that was the end of my singing career.*

On V-E Day in May 1945, they celebrated the end of the war in Europe at the NCO club. It was too hot to go in, so they sat outside drinking beer with two other couples they knew. They hushed at one point so Jane could sing. "She starts singing from 'Madame Butterfly,'" a song in which the Japanese geisha pines for her unfaithful American husband. She's sure that one day he'll return to her. "She was terrific. What a voice. She could have been a pro."

Jane invited him to her house for dinner on his twenty-first birthday. Her mother, Winnie, didn't like the idea at all. "She was maybe five-foot-one, or five-foot-two, and worked in the propeller shops. Ever see a two-bladed prop on an AT-6? It's a huge thing"—about nine feet tall. "She would balance it. That was her job," he said with admiration.

Over dinner, Winnie asked, "Are you a Jew, Pincus?"

"Yes," he said.

"Are you white?"

"Yes. My history goes back six thousand years."

"At that, Jane squeezed my wrist under the table—*keep your mouth shut.* OK, I can show them that a Yankee can be a gentleman. That's what they used to call me—Yankee."

She asked him if he knew the other Jews in town, a family that ran a shoe store. Schreiber's was on Main Street, next door to the Crystal Pharmacy. They sold ladies' shoes, sportswear, and fine jewelry. "If Mr. Schreiber couldn't fit you and find a style of shoe you liked," people said, "you might as well resign yourself to going barefoot." Surely, he knew them—didn't all Jews know each other? No, he didn't know the Schreibers. He was, I'm sure, the first New York Jew she had ever met. "Nice people," he said many years later, smiling, "although her mother didn't understand Jews."

Georgia in the 1940s may have been more foreign to him than England. The Army should have given New Yorkers a guide like the one they produced about how to understand British culture. This one could be called *So You're Headed to Dixie*. Another guide could have been written for southerners headed north: *So You're Meeting a Yankee*. (Or: *Your First Jew: What to Say. What Not to Say.*) However, the Army was a little too busy at the time to referee regions.

Jane was not deterred by her family's attitude. They kept seeing each other. She wanted him to get a three-day pass so they could go to Atlanta and get a hotel room. "Jane kept using two words in our conversation. One was called the M-word—that's M for marriage, and the other word, the C-word, C to convert." One time she had an important question.

> We're sitting around the table, munching on a sandwich and she said to me—she proposed to me. I said, "Are you serious?" I said. "Get married?" I said. "I'm only twenty years old."
>
> And she said, "I didn't realize that. You're so mature," she said. "It's just a number. It doesn't mean anything," she said, "I know what's bothering you. I'll convert."
>
> I said, "Don't worry about it. My plans for the future, right now—I'm very flattered that you even thought about it—right now I've got my mind on getting into a college and taking engineering." I was doing some studying in the meantime. She sounded a little disappointed. I'm sure she was.

And what if he had married Jane in Georgia or Judith in England? Here we run into life's randomness. It's chance upon chance, plans that aren't, a predetermined free will. I have no further thoughts because I wouldn't have been.

Jane is the larger mystery. Online I find one photo of a woman in a long, light-colored dress sitting in front of a small band of about fifteen, the Spence Field Skylarks. Her legs and her arms are crossed. She looks like she's at the ready. Calling her a small-town girl is to miss everything. She's a bit blurred in this one black-and-white photo, the kind of glimpse you get of an express train racing through a railroad crossing, a rush and a blur. She was a woman ahead of her time—an airplane mechanic, a band leader, a woman who proposed marriage. I would have loved to have met her.

Only in his last years did I learn about his Georgia days. He talked briefly about this "girl he was going with." One day he called a company— one of those 1-800 numbers—to ask a question. A woman with a southern drawl answered. "I kept her on the line. She was so pleasant to listen to," he said. The past calling again.

His last act of war was an act of repatriation. He did finally design something. The major that he clerked for called him into the office. "He said, 'I noticed you palling around with this little dog. I think his name is Corporal.'" When he was 10 years old he had wanted a dog, but he couldn't convince his parents.

> *"Well, the people who own that dog want him shipped home."*
> *I said, "Yes sir, what can I do?"*
> *"Sit down and make up a drawing and I'll build him a cage so he can be shipped home properly."*
> *"Yes sir."*
> *So, I went out to the drawing board—they had one there—and designed and built a dog cage which was considerably larger than the dog. And I showed it to the major. He was very pleased and compli-mented me on it. They put Corporal in it—a little, runty mutt. His loyalty was to anyone who would feed him. They shipped him out.*

Corporal was going home, and so was my father.

> *They had what they call a numbering system making you eligible for discharge. And I had enough points. You got so many points for each medal, so many points for each year of service, and so many points for this and that. The more points you had, the sooner you could get out of the Army. So, when my turn came, I applied for and got my discharge.*

He was discharged on November 20, 1945.

He caught a ride on an airplane flying north. His Uncle Sammy, who had given him a trumpet in hopes that it would keep him alive stateside, picked him up at Mitchel Field on Long Island. He had survived the war without playing a note.

## COMING HOME

"Years went by and thank God the war ended. And many of us were shipped out to be discharged. I got out of the Army Air Force and went home and was really greeted by my sister, and my brother-in-law," he said. That's what we want to hear. The heroes return. Blue skies and tickertape parades. We want a sharp line between war and peace. In popular memory the end of WWII is condensed to V-J Day, to a sailor in Times Square in an ardent embrace. Prosperity and the boom of the 1950s await. But wars cast shadows.

Away, serving their country, most G.I.s thought they would be returning to a continuing economic depression—it was all they'd ever known—and to a country where others had profited from the war. They would have lost their place. Most thought there would be no work when they got home. In one survey, 79 percent of soldiers believed it would be difficult to get a good job after the war, and 56 percent thought they'd face a "widespread Depression."

The veterans also had complicated feelings about civilians—they didn't understand the war, they hadn't done enough. They'd just gone along with their lives. "At home I went to a football game—I've always enjoyed 'em. But all that life and gaiety and luxury—it just makes you so mad. I never even noticed half the game. I got madder and madder—even though I know they can't help it," one told a psychologist. And they didn't like "bastardly 4Fs" and the "stay-at-home soldiers" who hadn't seen combat. Why did they have to salute a green sergeant? They disdained Army formality.

My father came home and joined the "52/20 club." Veterans received twenty dollars a week in unemployment compensation for fifty-two weeks. (About $320 today.) That was the only income he had.

"I was looking for a job. Finding a job as a draftsman was close to impossible. They weren't building new things." Mentored by his friend, "the super-salesman," Hy, he tried selling many things, including pots and pans and party favors. He called on restaurants and would be shown the door. He went back to engineering. "So, I went around on lower Broadway on Park Row. I went down to this office building where I knew they had engineering offices and I saw drafting tables being delivered." He followed the movers upstairs to a firm and introduced himself. "I said, 'I'm seeking employment as a mechanical draftsman. Any openings?'"

Did he know about ship design? Sure, he said. His nautical resume was brief: he'd been on the Staten Island Ferry, the Hudson River Day Line, and a troopship returning to the states.

The boss called him over to a table. "So, the first thing he did, he rolled out the layout of a ship. He said, 'Do you know what this is?'

"'Of course I know what it is.' I lied. 'This is the prow, and this is the fantail.' I learned that from a friend of mine who was in the Navy. And I got away with it." He was hired. They were converting the S.S. *Brazil* back to a luxury liner from its wartime service as a troop ship. The first time he was down in the ship's hull, he had a hard time telling fore from aft. There was no frame of reference, he said.

After that he worked for a company planning to dig a new route bypassing the locks in the Panama Canal to shorten the travel time between the Gulf of Mexico and the Pacific. "They were designing a dredge. 'Mr. Mansfield, do you know what a dredge is?' 'Yes, it digs up mud to create channels.' Very good." Hired again. And so he resumed his life as a civilian.

# 3

# NOT TELLING

THREE YEARS AFTER MY FATHER'S DEATH, MY NEPHEW SCOTT MANS-
field surprised me with a short video he had recorded. It's just a few
minutes of a grandson talking to his grandfather who is sitting in his
wheelchair in the fluorescent-white light of a kitchen. Scott is standing.
It was strange to see the home place, to recall the disorder of the house in
its last years. It was a mess, but one that he was happy living in.

He's smiling, happy to see Scott. Looking at him after a lapse of
years, I can see how time has battered him. His voice is hoarse; his left
hand stands out as something gnarly and large, a big oak burr, a fungus
growing in the woods.

And after just a bit, the strangeness of being back in the kitchen fades
away. Scott's questions are good, instinctual, and, surprisingly in that
moment, dad gives him honest answers. He still refuses to talk in detail,
but his refusal here is clear.

"Do you remember the *Mary Harriet*?" Scott asks.

"Merry old, *Mary Harriet*. A big, fat"—he pauses—"sweetheart." He
is smiling. "A big fat, twin tail—how do you remember *Mary Harriet*?"

"You told me about her, before."

"Really?"

"What was she?"

"World War II," he says faintly, as if orienting himself. "That airplane
could fly better on three engines than the four that it had," he says with
a laugh.

*"Three turning, one burning." That's what we used to say about it. We'd come back—we'd be flying along on three engines and I think the pilot or the copilot would shoot a flare. Wounded aboard. I could look out my window, I could see them peeling off in front of me, giving us the right of way. We landed without incident. These two guys who flew the airplane were super, great guys.*

"Was that the only one that you were in overseas?"

"No," he says. He also flew on *Her Man.* "On the side of the airplane it had a picture of a bull, a bull's head. It wasn't painted camouflage color. It was all silver. It was one of the latest—it had closed-in windows. The *Mary Harriet* had all open ports. You could stick your hand outside."

"Was it cold up there?"

"Thirty-eight below zero is the last number I remember. The first time I went up in the airplane I took along a canteen of juice. I think it was pineapple juice. I took it along. I figured I'd have a cold drink. It can get very dry. So on the way back I decided I'd have a drink. Nothing but a chunk of ice."

He pauses. His memories are taking him away. "It was quite an adventure. I was even able to speak then without a hoarse throat."

"Did you ever talk to any of the guys from the war afterwards?"

"No. No," he says quickly. "I have a thing in my head about that. Because I didn't want to talk about the war. It's all over. Because we thought we were doing what we had to. And I didn't—to be quite frank—I knew we were killing people. And of course that's not the way I was brought up." He raises his voice as if he were in an argument: "But it was either them or me. It was going to be them. That was the way I looked at it."

In that one statement, he's caught in a riptide of emotions—*I didn't want to kill; I had to kill.* On one of the tapes he had sent to me, he was talking about how the other boys used to taunt him about his bad hand and how his mother used to lecture him before he went out to play.

*She would say, "If you get into a fight, make sure you give back." I remembered those words many years later when I was in the Army Air Force and I stood by my window at my gun position and watched the bombs fall over Germany. I thought to myself, "I'm giving back, Ma. I'm giving back," as we dropped thousands of pounds of TNT.*

This is like nothing else he ever said. He didn't speak badly of other people, except to say that a certain mechanic was a "chiseler" or that so-and-so was a "gonif," a thief. That sort of thing. But did he really feel that way as the bombs fell over Germany? Probably not. In the moment, as we say today, the moment was overwhelming.

His friends, the Five Guys from the Bronx, went off to the Army, the Army Air Forces, and the Navy. They all came home after the war. No one talked about it. His friend Hy served in the Pacific. "Where were you?" they asked him. "New Guinea," he answered, and other than to say that he hated it, he never mentioned it again. He was friends with Hy for another fifty years. Not one word passed between them about the war.

Whenever anyone asked him about the war, he told them, "It's over for crying out loud. Get on with it," he said. "I'd rather talk about the job I was doing and about my new friends here on (Long) Island." He changed the subject and began talking about his friends. That's all the war story we were gonna' get from him.

Once, after Thanksgiving dinner, a relative was talking about a jury he'd served on, a particularly upsetting case of sexual assault. The trial had been in the headlines for weeks. The case had hinged on some intimate details not publicly reported, and our relative, without prompting, freely spilled what had been left out of the newspapers.

All the way home my father was upset. I hadn't seen him that angry since the days when I got into kid trouble growing up. "He should have never said that," my father said. "Why did he have to say that? He knows better." He was almost the same age as my father, and also a veteran. These were the only cross words he'd spoken about this man.

This was the code, an unspoken code about what is said and what is not. This mattered greatly to my father and the men of his generation. The ugly things you had seen in the war, and what you felt about that, all that was left unsaid.

## VETERANS HOME

Ten years after the war ended, my father and mother, along with my older brother David, moved into the first and only house our family would live in. It was a small house, the bare minimum to join suburbia—three bedrooms, one bathroom, one picture window, one narrow garage. In all just seven or eight hundred square feet on a small lot, but for me, like all childhood homes, it contained the universe.

They had moved into a new house while they were still young and everyone around them was young, and the entire landscape was waiting to be rewritten. The houses sat bare and barracks-like on the flatness of the vanished Long Island potato field. They looked thin, boxy, and vulnerable.

He loved that house. It was, in our childhood, a great project. He was an avid handyman in an era of can-do home-improvers. And in its last years, the old home was a comfortable mess. He was living alone by the time he was getting into his nineties. My mother was in a nursing home. He visited her weekly, along with David, who lived nearby and looked after him. He also had help come in, but he was still alone a worrying amount. He'd lost much of his eyesight to macular degeneration and had to use a walker and a wheelchair to get around.

Small and large emergencies broke out, falling upon my brother, sometimes in the lean hours after midnight when any emergency is magnified. He had a serious fall that sent him to rehab at the hospital for weeks, and then a year or so later, another fall, another call to an ambulance, and another tour of rehab. Our father's solo life, help and all, was taking its toll on my brother.

We had the agonized, painful discussion faced by many families about extinguishing the independence of their parents. Should he go to a nursing home? This was a hard bridge to cross, but we did it. We managed to get him on the waiting list at the Veterans Home, and into the home. We had visited with my father. I have been in enough nursing homes to calculate the levels of grim neglect and despair, but the Vets Home was bright and cheerful with an active, engaged staff. It was a good fit; he loved the place.

At the home, many of the other men were wearing crisp, new military ballcaps. The Navy guys had their ship names stitched in gold thread; a wheelchair-bound Marine wore a cap that said Iwo Jima. On the back of the caps, in case you had missed it, was embroidered "Army Veteran" or just "Veteran." My father wore a dirty Yankees ballcap—his first posting, the Bronx. He was born there and growing up he lived at several addresses he still remembered. (1281 Clinton Ave., 2074 Arthur Ave., 1271 Grant Ave., 1075 Kelly St., and 1639 Monroe Ave.) When he was first married they had an apartment on Nelson Avenue. On summer Saturday afternoons when the windows were open they could hear the cheers at the stadium. They would run to turn on the radio, but by the time the tubes had warmed up, it was too late to hear about the diving catch, the home run, the throw to second to get the runner. In the Atlantic City convention center, at the *Repple Depple*, he saw this big man in an expensive blue suit sitting on a table. "The tall guy looked very familiar." He went over to him. It was Joe DiMaggio, the Yankee Clipper. Joltin' Joe said hello. My father was speechless. "I was thunderstruck that I had actually seen Joe DiMaggio in person."

He did have a few small complaints about the Vets Home. "Everyone wants to talk about the war and what you did in the war—*Who cares*," he said. He attended many of the programs, except the music. "All they play is military music." They took the vets to a minor league baseball game. The ballpark put their names on the scoreboard; the crowd stood to applaud them. "You should have seen the fuss they made over us," he said in disbelief. It was too much; he brushed it off. When his grandsons were admiring a picture of him at nineteen in his Air Force uniform, he replied "Just a stupid kid in his uniform." And another time he said, "Nineteen, and off to kill people." Sometimes I think he was a closet pacifist.

Some of the old vets began to talk forty to fifty years later. Not my father. They held small reunions. My father would have never gone—even if the reunion was in his living room. He knew that his pilot, Carl Vail Jr., had a car dealership out East on the Island, but he never went to see him. He had mentioned this when I was young. Let's go see him, I said. My dad liked cars and liked to drive out there now and again. But he had no interest. Why? He gave no answer.

Some vets flew to England and walked the ruins of the old airfields. The old men, stepping with care off the big tour buses, some with wives beside them, others with sons and daughters and grandchildren, looked about, trying to locate the vanished runways, barracks, and airfield tower. They were in search of what was absent. They wanted to report, "This is how it was," but sixty years and more had gone by. They had been part of something big, but what was it?

This was another Mars landing, a journey across great distance to land where nothing was named. The airfields had been plowed back to grow sugar beets and potatoes and raise cattle. Some huts remained, home to pigs or crumbling under the trees. The visitors from across the years looked at the tumbled concrete steps of 1944, another ruin in the landscape, joining the Neolithic stone circles, eighth-century earthworks, twelfth-century castles, and fourteenth-century abbeys.

They had to confront what was missing—the men who didn't make it home. They wouldn't be at the PTA, the Elks Lodge, the wedding altar. They wouldn't marry, divorce, prosper, fail. They wouldn't be there for their daughter's science fair, their son's school play. They didn't get to grow old. They were gone in their youth. It's this absence that may be the hardest to face, the spaces all around of unlived lives.

Young men die in war and old men, years later, are left to wonder at the cruelty of that killing. All the old-man memoirs say, "Somehow, I'm here."

The men around us—the ones mowing lawns and coaching Little League had seen some terrible things. And they came home while others—their friends and comrades, sometimes just inches from them—had been killed. Veteran was another name for survivor.

They were silent about what they had seen. Their silence spoke of what the writer Edie Clark calls "what there was not to tell." Her father served almost four years in Europe and Africa and came home to report that "there isn't much to tell." She never heard her father say, "When I was in the war."

This "not telling" was a big part of the post-war years. The big war was constantly in movies, on TV, in books, and in the toy guns we played war with, and yet so much was left unsaid. As Walt Whitman said of the Civil War, "the real war will never get in the books." He had nursed the Union wounded in Washington. He knew the real war.

I remember a TV show that we saw only once, *12 O'clock High*, based on a best-selling novel and a movie about B-17 bomber crews flying out of England. The movie was celebrated and watched for years in the Air Force's leadership training. This was the story of the Eighth Air Force at war—my father's war—in different airplanes and in battles before he was over there. But he had no patience for the show. That's not how it was, he said. Why? we asked. The actors are too old, is all he said and nothing more. He wouldn't explain. He wouldn't watch, and he didn't want us watching it either, and this was when most parents let their kids watch just about anything.

The big war was everywhere in the 1950s and 1960s, and yet elusive. Millions of men and women had gone through it, but who got to speak about it, and how the war was presented—the stories that were told—is puzzling to me.

They kept their demons to themselves. "War happens inside a man. It happens to one man alone. It can never be communicated," said Eric Sevareid, a CBS radio correspondent who covered World War II. "That's the tragedy—and perhaps the blessing. . . . And, I am sorry to say, that is also why in a certain sense you and your sons from the war will be forever strangers." It was a *world* war—it happened in thousands of places to millions of men, women, and children. The soldier, the airman, is only one guy landing on the beach, in a tank, in the air, in his tent or barracks. One guy sent here and there. One war happening millions of times.

The war was everywhere when I grew up, but most of it was unspoken. I was a child living on top of an iceberg. World War II was omnipresent; it was invisible. The real war will never get in the books.

Most veterans entered peacetime like the commander of the 453rd, Ramsay Potts. He was a leader in the costly raid on the Ploesti oil refinery, flew forty-one combat missions, and later commanded two different bomber groups before moving on to the staff of the Eighth Air Force as Director of Bombing Operations. Potts came home as a colonel and put the war away. "It was decades after the war before I felt like I wanted to talk about it. I think the experience was so profound and the danger so great that you'd feel when talking to people who hadn't experienced it that maybe they'll think I'm exaggerating, maybe they'll think I'm bragging, maybe they'll think I'm trying to make this out to be more than it really was. But the fact of the matter is that it was an extremely dangerous, hazardous task every damned day you went on one of these missions. You could even say that to some extent you were exposed to danger on the ground at your base because the Germans would try to launch some kind of attack on the bases in England."

## THEY SHALL ALWAYS BE WITH YOU

The writer James Salter was a fighter pilot in the Korean War, chasing Russian MIGs over North Korea and sometimes into China. After the war, he stayed in the Air Force, flying jets in Europe. Salter loved the Air Force. "I ate and drank it, went in whatever weather on whatever day, talked its endless talk, climbed on the wing to fuel the ship myself." His squadron, one routine weekend, lost a pilot. Two men were off to Chateauroux on a weekend jaunt. The ground crew had checked the jets, certifying them as good to go, but they had neglected to check the oil. Over France, one pilot, DeShazer, was suddenly in trouble—flames shooting out the tailpipe. His engine had seized up. He ejected, but his seat was defective. Deshazer, his "arms fluttering wildly," fell and fell, his parachute streaming out late, never fully blooming, before he hit the trees.

Salter didn't know him well—he was "homely, balding, with widely spaced teeth"—and Salter would never forget him. "An accident occurring in another squadron seemed a consequence of some kind; in one's own squadron it was fate, heavy and humbling. The days became divided, those before and those to come." Deshazer, "with his wide, cracked-lip smile would remain in one's life. Arms flapping, he would tumble endlessly, his parachute, long and useless, trailing behind. Not at first, and not until you accept that you are mortal, do you begin to realize that life and death are the same thing."

I don't know who remained in my father's memories, or in the memories of the men up and down the block, men who were home from the Navy, the Marines, and the Army. Soon it was ten years later, 1955, then 1965, and onward the years spun. World War II was the big object in the landscape, and as the years passed, it seemed that it could be seen less and less. It was codified in images and words: The Greatest Generation, The Good War; and in a select roll call of battles: the Battle of Britain, D-Day, the liberation of Paris, the Battle of the Bulge, the Bridge at Remagen, and, in the Pacific, Pearl Harbor, Guadalcanal, Iwo Jima, Okinawa.

Here I was growing up in a suburb built by the veterans—Veterans' Memorial Island as I thought of it—with its Veterans Memorial Highway, Veterans Memorial Coliseum, Veterans Memorial Playing Field, and the war became, over time, a big blank wall on which flashed Hollywood movies and a few big novels, but mostly the silent spaces of what there was not to tell.

On Memorial Days, where I grew up, the VFW opened its doors to everyone. They gave out free hot dogs, which to us boys was a bonanza. We were all in. We swooped in on our banana-seat bikes. The VFW was in a small ranch house they must have built in the 1950s. The inside, as I recall, was one big room. It was a bar. This post of the VFW was a drinking club. "You know," we said to each other, "it's just a bar."

Some men came home and filled out their old uniforms just as they filled out their war stories, becoming drunk Odysseus's at the VFW bar, sitting there talking about it again and again until the memories were calloused and closed. But most veterans returned, tossed their uniforms, and never marched on Memorial Day or Veterans Day. But this didn't mean they didn't remember.

The Air Force had trained them to fly, to aim guns and bombs, to take apart a Browning .50 caliber machine gun blindfolded, to fix a 1,200 horsepower Pratt & Whitney air-cooled radial aircraft engine, to fly in close formation with other bombers, to look through the Norden bombsight while calculating altitude, heading, wind speed, and direction. But no one had trained them to understand killing.

My father's leaving the war in Europe was a gift, of sorts. The United States Strategic Bombing Survey shouldn't be a bedtime story. Forgetting is a tragedy and a blessing, as Sevareid had said. But it's a costly gift. No one gets to live outside of history.

I walked clear through a B-24 once. It had been restored by a foundation and was being flown around to various airports. I knew it wasn't a true war report—it was clean and empty—no bombs, no guns, no ammo, no ten men in their bulky gear and oxygen masks, no 38 degrees below zero, no fear.

This scrubbing of the past often happens in museums, the life drained out of the art, objects, and houses that have been saved. The treasure is arrested in time. I've visited restored historic farms without a whiff of hay or manure—smelling vaguely perfumed. I don't doubt that the bomber was technically correct, but that's seldom the whole story.

But, wow, was it small inside—even without the bombs, guns, and crew. It was like a submarine with every nut and bolt and seam exposed.

I told my father that I'd been aboard a B-24 and thought it was small. He was surprised. "We thought it was a big airplane," he said.

Something that could fly ten men and carry tons of bombs 1,700 miles was big when compared to what came before. More than a dozen years before, a slender, single-engine airplane carried one man and 450 gallons of fuel across the Atlantic to a triumphant reception in Paris, and in an instant in 1927 made him the most famous man on earth—Charles Lindbergh, Lucky Lindy.

In its pristine state, the restored B-24 was like our memory of the war—the war part mostly expunged, and the size of the war reduced to a manageable attraction landing one Saturday at an airport near you.

## FORGETTING THE OLD COUNTRY

My father was continuing our family tradition of *not* telling. Other families have family historians; we have family *ahistorians*. (Though all family histories are an exercise in selective telling, an exercise in choosing your ancestors. Uncle John is us; Uncle Barry—no, not at all, an aberration. Don't speak his name. Selective telling. All family histories are a forgetting.)

His parents, Elai and Ida, were immigrants from the same shtetl. They never spoke of the "Old Country." I had gathered, after persistent questioning, a meager outline. At age 20 Elai left his village of Smorgon near Vilna in Lithuania—or Poland or Russia—it kept changing landlords—where Jews were restricted, allowed to live in only a few places, allowed only a few jobs. Elai's parents had died from pneumonia and what little property the family owned had been confiscated. The Czar was looking for "recruits." In a few months Russia would enter World War I. He left. A draft dodger, you could say. He walked across Europe, sleeping in barns and begging for food at farmhouses, and somewhere along the way, changing his last name. He made it to Germany, was sponsored by a family and shipped to America out of Hamburg, arriving in New York City on February 6, 1914.

Elai's brother, Hillel, stayed behind. For years Elai and Ida sent him money for his passage to America. They urged him to take his family and leave the Old Country. No, he wrote back, things are good here, our farm and our shoe repair shop are doing well. He put the money into the shop. They also sent food and coffee, which was buried so it wouldn't be stolen. One day the Nazis walked into his village and killed everyone. A common story. Elai and Ida got the news and never spoke of it again.

This was how it was *not* told in the family. We didn't tell stories. I had asked and the answer was shorthand, just a few sentences. The aim was to tell the story as briefly as possible. My grandparents surrounded the Old Country with a deep silence. I swear they could have been the guardians of nuclear secrets. They never would have told a soul.

The history was more extensive and worse. The Nazis arrived in June 1941, began rounding up the Jews, sending them to the ghettos and death camps. Hillel's life ended when he was forty-seven years old, in 1942 in Ponary, Poland. From 1941 to 1944 in the Ponary Massacre, seventy thousand Jews were murdered and buried in mass graves.

"He was called Handsome Hillel by all the ladies who ever met him. I saw his picture and it was true. He was a good-looking guy," said my father. "Anyway, he perished in the Holocaust. And this upset my father no end." Hillel had three sons and a daughter. One son, Shlomo, escaped going to Romania first, then to Israel.

I looked up this history recently, and the date stood out: The Nazis removed the Jews from Smorgon in summer 1942. A year later my father was in the Army Air Forces.

∞

As we came out of the pandemic, a young reporter, Emma Green, went to talk to Dr. Ruth Westheimer, the sex advice guru. Dr. Ruth, a ninety-three-year-old widow, lived in her neighborhood. The famous doctor had faced the lockdown alone and got through by talking to her friends daily on the phone. Dr. Ruth loved giving big dinner parties and going out with her many friends. She couldn't leave her apartment. The pandemic was a lonely time.

Green, in her early thirties, told her that she was feeling out of sorts and strange, as she began to see people again.

Dr. Ruth surprised her. Don't dwell on it, she said. Get out there. Make plans, move on. "You think we're just going to move on and leave it behind?" Green asked.

"Absolutely. And that's what I subscribe to."

"Really?"

"Yes."

"One thing that I hear people talking about is this idea that it's hard to go back to normal right now," Green said.

"That what?"

"It's hard to go back to normal life, because people feel like they've lived through something traumatic."

"People feel what?"

"That they've lived through something traumatic."

"I'm going to say to people, 'Stop constantly talking about how difficult it was.' We all know that. Period. Just have that *joie de vivre*, that joy of life, in—in your heart. You're not going to forget this year."

"Sure."

"But—but stop harping on it."

Dr. Ruth was orphaned by the Holocaust. When she was 10 years old, she had watched the Gestapo load her father into a truck to take him to the Dachau concentration camp. A few weeks later her mother and grandmother, fearing for Ruth's future, put her on a train, a *kinder-transport*, headed to a Swiss orphanage. She would never see her father, mother, or grandmother again. They perished in the death camps. For the rest of her childhood, no one ever hugged her. From Switzerland, Dr. Ruth went to Israel where she fought as a sniper in the war for independence. She was severely wounded by an exploding shell in a mortar attack, almost losing her feet. Temporarily paralyzed, she spent months recuperating before she could walk. She went on to study at the Sorbonne in Paris, and eventually to America, working as a maid to put herself through graduate school. It took her years to get past thinking that if she had stayed in Germany she could have saved her parents. She had to overcome the "irrational guilt" of a survivor.

Green realized that Dr. Ruth is "focused relentlessly on *living*—not lingering on the past, but just being totally energized in every moment of the present." She, too, was an *ahistorian*, a skilled practitioner of what there was not to tell. The Old Country was an ocean away and every day was a new day that took her farther from the war. The past is another country, is the old saying. We don't live there.

## THE FIRE

I can't look up my father's war record. The same is true for about 17 million other Army and Air Force veterans who served between 1912 and 1963. The papers listing his training, promotions, and awards, the "201" as it is known, is gone, lost in flames.

Just after midnight on July 12, 1973, the sixth floor of the National Personnel Records Center in St. Louis was on fire. Fire engines were there four minutes and twenty seconds after the first call, but the fire was out of control and would burn for the next twenty-two hours. Forty-one additional fire districts joined the first fire company. The fire was finally declared out after four days. They had managed to keep the fire to the sixth floor, saving the Navy and Marine records on other floors. But the fire destroyed about 80 percent of the Army and Air Force records. The fire was so hot that metal shelving and filing cabinets twisted and buckled. All that remained of most files were sodden ashes. The archives looked like it had been bombed. Out of fire, more fire. Out of destruction, ever more destruction. Peace, too, but a destruction that can never be healed.

The fire is sadly symbolic of the way time and the culture consume the memories of war. The fire took all the details about induction, training, battles fought, medals won, wounds, and death. The fire wiped away the real story. As the World War II vets die, it's like another fire. There are memoirs, histories, and monuments, of course, and Hollywood movies without end, but the real war will never get into the public memory.

The B-24 also disappeared. After the war, the B-24, the most numerous American warplane, was scrapped, cut up, and left to rot on Pacific islands. More B-24s had been built than any other American airplane in the brief span of aviation history. In August 1945 there were 4,236 of the ugly, tubby but tough airplanes in the Army Air Forces. Two years later at the start of the Air Force as an independent military branch, there were zero. If you see a WWII bomber in any movie about the war in Europe, it's always the slimmer, better-looking B-17. It just looks the part.

The airmen who flew the B-24 were loyal to the plane they flew into battle. When I first looked up my father's plane, *The Mary Harriet*, the first Google search brought up two photos and the information that it had crashed in Switzerland—after his time, I had assumed. The *Mary Harriet* was hit by flak while bombing an armaments factory near Munich. It limped to Switzerland. The entire crew, except one, parachuted to safety. The plane went down somewhere between Zurich and Innsbruck. The underground later returned the pilot and copilot to England.

When I told him that I'd found photos of the *Mary Harriet*, he couldn't believe it. "The *Mary Harriet*? There's a picture of it?" He lived computer free; to him Google was just a funny word. Then I told him that it had crashed. "The *Mary Harriet* crashed?" He took this hard, as if it had just happened. This news upset him.

I was wrong. I had the wrong airplane. I'd made a rookie mistake. I hadn't checked the serial number. But I was surprised by his concern for a machine he had last seen when he was twenty years old. In that moment time flexed, and 1944 was only yesterday.

## REMORSE

I have a nephew who lives in Germany. Eric went to Germany first as a student and returned to work there. Before he left on his first trip, my brother brought him to say goodbye to his "Poppa Pincus and Grandma Bernice."

"The first thing I remember him saying was that Berlin was famous for its tree-lined boulevards like Unter den Linden," said Eric. "He also told me that he felt very sad about the large numbers of civilian deaths caused by the Allied aerial bombings on the cities and that war was a terrible thing. He never said to me anything against the Nazis, modern Germany, or the German people."

On parting, he told his grandson, "Don't tell them what your grandfather did to their beautiful country."

Most of the men in the bombers "could not tolerate well the guilt of killing," said an Air Force psychiatric study of the first year of combat. "Even though in aerial warfare the victims are remote, almost abstract," said the study, seemingly surprised. The distance of bombing is always emphasized—dropping a bomb from 20,000 feet and winging your way home. But the killing had marked them. "The specter of . . . the extermination of innocents would forever lie in the back of my mind as I matured," said Bernard Thomas Nolan, a pilot in the 487th BG.

They could see what was left out of the official reports. Sgt. John J. Briol was a ball turret gunner on a B-17 in 457th BG. He was part of a mission on January 2, 1944, to bomb the railroad yards at the center of Mayen. In the Plexiglas and steel ball protruding from the bottom of the fuselage, he had a clear view. "This was a little city of about two thousand people. We blasted the yards alright and the entire city with it. I saw the whole city disappearing and I suddenly realized again what a rotten business this was."

It wasn't only a few airmen who had a clear view. After the Allied victory in Europe, Gen. Jimmy Doolittle ordered the Eighth Air Force to fly the supporting workers—mechanics, cooks, typists—around Europe to see what they had done. Close to 48,000 men flew on these "trolley runs," low-level flights that were an extensive sightseeing tour of bombed out factories, railroad yards, and cities: Frankfurt, looking "like Pompeii magnified"; Kassel, "just miles of rust staring to the sky"; Leuna, "an enormous desert of iron skeletons"; Magdeburg, "another ghost city," Bruce C. Hopper, chief historian for the Eighth Air Force, wrote of his own, earlier tour. Many of the forty thousand left in Cologne hung on in cave-like coal cellars, scavenging for food in foul-smelling piles of rubble, fending off "insolent and fat" rats that lived on decaying corpses. After walking the wasteland that was Cologne, Lt. Kenneth "Deacon" Jones said, "I was 20 years old and felt ancient."

Doolittle's "trolley runs" were a grim harvest, rousing, in some, a strong aversion to killing. Studies of armies in the field are surprising in revealing how much soldiers *didn't* want to kill. They felt guilty about not shooting and didn't talk about it. An influential, pioneering study by Gen. S.L.A. Marshall found that only 15 to 20 percent of World War II infantrymen in combat fired their guns. This was not unusual. At Gettysburg, nearly 90 percent of the 27,574 muskets that were collected from the battlefield were loaded, some many times. Men, standing up, vulnerable, went through the motions of loading, but avoided firing. In the midst of the war's biggest battle, they performed a pantomime. In World War I, soldiers were relieved when they were ordered to a quieter sector, not so much for their own safety, but because they were no longer "under the compulsion to take life," said Marshall. In World War II, less than 1 percent of fighter pilots were responsible for 30 to 40 percent of enemy airplanes destroyed. Most fighter pilots didn't shoot or even try. This is not the story we usually hear. "It is only heroes and the glory that make their way into print," says former Army Ranger Dave Grossman. We are fed tales of Rambo and others like him "blithely and remorselessly killing off men by the hundreds."

Remorse is borne quietly by veterans like Frank Devita, who was nineteen, part of a three-man crew piloting a landing craft on D-Day through fifteen trips. On his first landing, he opened the gate with great reluctance and fifteen men were gunned down. One died right next to him, gripping his hand.

*The kid that was standing next to me, the machine gun took his helmet off, and part of his head. He had red hair. And he was crying, "Help me. Help me." I had no morphine. I couldn't help him—I couldn't help him. And he kept crying, "Help me. Help me." I had nothing in my arsenal. So, I prayed. I started saying the Our Father. And when I prayed, he stopped screaming "Help me. Help me." And I don't know what possessed me. I reached down. I squeezed his hand. He squeezed my hand as if to say, "It's alright." And he died—he died. We had 90 percent casualties on the first wave. And then we turned around and did it again.*

That night, back aboard the ship, Frank Devita, a teenager, cried himself to sleep.

And it's borne by veterans like James McEachin, a Korean War vet, who shot a soldier in Korea long ago in a war mostly forgotten—but he never forgets. "The first time I shot somebody he was walking on the ridgeline and I had a clear shot at him and it was almost like slow motion," says McEachin. "There was a god-awful silence and that was my first encounter. I don't know if I ever recovered from it." It doesn't leave you, they all say.

Nicholas Irving was a Special Operations Sniper with the Army Rangers serving in Iraq and Afghanistan. He was deadly, credited with thirty-three kills on one tour and nicknamed "the Reaper." He lived by the sniper's motto: "without warning, without remorse." Well, Irving says, "I don't know how you're not supposed to have remorse." He is haunted by nightmares in which he sees the first man he ever killed.

In all those Memorial Day and Veteran's Day speeches and editorials, is there ever remorse? No. You don't hear it.

Seventy-five years after he went to war, my father sat with a tape recorder alone in his kitchen, in the twenty-first century, making up stories. And one was a war story. He broke his own prohibition again.

The story is set in October 1944, at a bomber base in England. A crew is flying its twentieth mission when they are hit by flak. He was hit on his nineteenth mission in October 1944. The story proceeds like a reenactment, precise enough to be a training film. This story, too, is told entirely in dialogue. The pilot is talking, issuing instructions.

"Everybody into the airplane and good luck to all of us," he says. "Tighten your parachute harness; check all your positions, your oxygen, your guns. We do not take off with hot guns. . . . Check for other aircraft. . . . We're coming up on 10,000 feet. Get ready to put your oxygen mask on. And make sure your control is set at automix, off. Everybody ready? Good. Remember if we're attacked, short bursts on your machine gun." And then, "Here comes the flak, men. Put on your apron, your armor apron.

"We're hit—not too badly, but there goes Number One engine. It's starting to throw white smoke." The pilot tells the flight engineer, Tommie, to "set up all three engines to fly this airplane." The flight engineer had to have technical savvy and act fast in an emergency. If a bomber lost an engine, he would isolate that engine, shift the fuel flow, and try to contain any fire. "Everybody on the alert. Look out for intervening aircraft. We don't need any company." They reach the target, but one bomb gets stuck. Tommie goes to the bomb bay to free it. They'll drop it over the water. A fighter attacks. "Twelve o'clock high? Alright. Short bursts, remember men." There's more flak.

The co-pilot, Charlie, is hit, "bleeding like a pig." Refusing help, Charlie makes a tourniquet. Nearing their airfield, they fire a red flare to get priority in landing and alert the ambulance. They land. "Here comes an ambulance. Alright, everybody stay alert and give him a hand."

It turns out there are two wounded. The pilot has been hit in the leg, though less seriously than his co-pilot. But there's a twist to the story. Co-pilot Charlie is Black. He trained with the Tuskegee Airmen. This never happened. The air crews were all white, except for close to one thousand Black airmen who served in their own units, including the famous 332nd Fighter Group, and a Black bomber crew. There were no integrated crews.

The ambulance crew tries to take Charlie to a segregated hospital ward. The pilot won't allow it. "Hey! Where are you going with that man?

Just because he's colored you're going to put him in a different section? You put him right here! You've got your orders? This pistol I'm carrying tells me you've got your orders from me. You put him next to me in the ward. You understand? Signify by saying yes." Charlie is put in the ward, "bleeding terrible," right next to his pilot.

He's set up a good story about respect and sacrifice in war. But the tape abruptly stops with half the side blank, left to unwind with a hiss, like a tire losing air. He turns away from two stories—the one he's telling and the memory of his own injury. Silence. Did he sit there in the kitchen a long while or go and watch TV, flipping through the channels?

He was thinking about his nineteenth mission. I think he regretted that he couldn't complete a full tour of thirty-five missions. Carl Vail Jr., the pilot, finished his tour and was home by early December to get married. Harry Haney, the "old man" navigator, would stay to fly an astonishing seventy-two missions over Europe and have a career in the Air Force as a major, before he died at age 56 from heart failure.

Finishing things was important to him. Growing up, I was taught to finish whatever I'd started. I remember laboring for hours over the multiplication table in third grade. I can still see the "times table" in the *World Book Encyclopedia*, its shiny page smudged by my finger trying to decode the inscrutable numbers: 8 × 4, 8 × 5. . . . Checking my homework, he'd tell me to go back and try again. You need "stick-to-ativity-ness," he'd say. "Try and try again." That's how he got through, by working hard.

His hand was the visible sign of his toughness, a word I didn't associate with him when he was alive. He was tough—but not a tough guy at all. He never boasted, never struck a tough-guy pose.

But at the end of his life, I added it up: a bad car accident in his early twenties, just after the war. The head-on crash when I was in the tenth grade. He was in the front passenger seat in a Volkswagen. The car collapsed around him. He was in the hospital for weeks. My brother David, who had just gotten his driver's license, stepped up to keep things going at home. Numerous small operations on his hand that he never mentioned. "*It's nothing. An inconvenience.*" Colon cancer in his late sixties and, years later, two falls at home, followed by rehab and recovery. And yet he was on only one minor medication in his last years. He'd lost most of his sight by then. How much? More than he let on. He also had a hard time walking and was more and more in a wheelchair. He was tough.

Growing up he didn't finish everything. No one does. At age 12, "I took my bar mitzvah lessons and was scheduled to make a speech at the end of the ceremony in English, Yiddish, and Hebrew. And the rabbi would come and sit with my father and listen to me practice it, and I had it down pat." His father thought his son might become a rabbi. "And then, as luck would have it, I got so sick, from what, I don't know. I couldn't appear for the bar mitzvah, and I couldn't make my speech. Disappointed my father for years to come, but I was forgiven later when I joined the Army Air Force."

One more story that I came across late, three years after he had died: I was helping my brother sort out boxes of family photos and a few other things left over from the old house. There were two microcassettes that he had recorded a decade earlier and put away. One tape was very short, just a few minutes. His voice is serious. He speaks carefully, as if he were testifying in court. He begins, "October 1944. I was a staff sergeant, Unites States Army, part of the Eighth Air Force stationed in England. I was an aerial gunner and part of a bomber crew on a B-24 Liberator bomber." In a handful of sentences, he talks about watching, on different missions, a B-17 blow up mid-air, a B-24 ditch in the water with its fate unknown, and another B-24 on fire as the men jumped. He counted the parachutes. He had told a war story and he quickly set it aside, saying again, "And that's all the war story I'm gonna tell you."

He pauses and continues.

*But now I'm gonna tell you another war story. The war was over. It was probably 1957 or '58. We were home sitting there, and Mom came in and said to me and David, a little guy about five or six years old, Mom said, "You two boys sit and watch television, I'm going to prepare supper." So, I put on the TV and little David and I are sitting and watching it. And they put on the newsreel and on the newsreel they showed pictures of bombers flying over cities, dropping bombs, and destroying homes. And they showed the people below.*

*Mom came in and said to little David, she said, "You see that airplane there, that's the airplane your father flew in the war." And they were watching these airplanes dropping bombs on the cities, destroying everything.*

*And David said to me, "Were there little boys there like me?"*

*I didn't know how to answer that question. What do you say? It was them or me. I was part of the war and I was only following orders. How do you answer a question like that to a five-year-old boy, five, six years old? I never knew how to answer that and to this day I don't know. It's just something I was never able to forget. And you can add that to my biography if you so desire.*

## War in Peace

When victory came, it was haunted by the dead. There was dancing and relief. There was shouting in the street. But the veterans couldn't forget what they had seen and what they had done.

Ernie Pyle couldn't forget the sight of

*dead men by mass production—in one country after another—month after month and year after year. Dead men in winter and dead men in summer.*

*Dead men in such familiar promiscuity that they become monotonous.*

*Dead men in such monstrous infinity that you come almost to hate them.*

*Those are the things that you at home need not even try to understand. To you at home they are columns of figures, or he is a near one who went away and just didn't come back. You didn't see him lying so grotesque and pasty beside the gravel road in France.*

The veterans, our fathers and grandfathers, uncles and cousins, brought the dead home with them. That's what they could not say. It's what the men brooding at the bar in the VFW couldn't say, or tried to say, or tried to avoid saying. And what they wanted to say was: *Why did you send me to kill? Thou shalt not kill.*

My father, like most of the men of his generation, chose silence. It was just as Pyle had written—there "are the things that you at home need not even try to understand." By his silence, he said, I give you peace. Take it. Take the yawning days of summer boredom, the hours on the floor watching TV shows with a talking horse or a wily coyote, the hours lost with a coloring book on a rainy day; take the snow days that close school, days that are like finding a lucky penny; take the school plays and proms, touch football in the street, games of keep away and tag, days of play from sun up to sundown. Take it all. I give you peace. Take it and don't ask me for more. I will tell no war stories.

# POSTSCRIPT
## Over Long Island Sound

Private pilot, c. 1970.

Twenty-three years after he had been carried off the *Mary Harriet* on a stretcher he was back in the sky, this time as a pilot. He joined the flying club at work, took lessons, soloed, and surprised us with the news. "I thought I had enough flying in World War II, but I never controlled an airplane and always wondered about it," he said.

I flew with him around the Long Island skies, flew across the Sound, flew to Spring Valley, New York, to see one of his old childhood friends, and flew from Syracuse when he'd flown in to take me home after Freshman year. That was the last time I was in the co-pilot's seat. Tired from exams and term papers, I slept most of the way. I wish I could say that I awoke, took the controls, and we soared through the air, a Hollywood ending. But no.

I never really enjoyed flying with him. He was a tense aviator, so it seemed to me. All good pilots are careful. They are tuned to the hum of the engine, what the instruments say, and any twitch in the weather—*There are old pilots and bold pilots, but no old, bold pilots.* Every pilot knows that. Good pilots are ready to react to an emergency with an instinct that they have schooled with every hour in their logbook. But his attention was of a higher, stricter order. It's how he learned to fly, first as a man with a machine gun.

His first one hundred hours in the air over Europe people were trying to kill him. He was a target. He'd seen all that he wouldn't talk about— fighters diving out of the sun, out of nowhere; bombers exploding, men disappearing into nowhere; anti-aircraft guns showering steel on the big bombers, on the *Mary Harriet*, wounding his crewmates, wounding him—so no wonder he might be hyper-vigilant when he took to the air put-putting around the blue skies of peacetime Long Island.

It wasn't PTSD; it was habit, it was training. "Watch for traffic," he always reminded me. The skies in the New York area are busy with other small planes and airliners above, but this was more like tracking the enemy. (Even so, that Cessna 150, two miles away, wasn't going to turn and run at us from two o'clock, with its 30mm canons firing.)

And he'd always have me looking for emergency landing fields—again, a standard flying practice, but ratcheted up. How about that sod farm? *Yes—no, wait—power lines—No, I think you could stick a short-field landing.*

Crossing the Long Island Sound—twenty-one miles wide—echoed crossing the English Channel—also twenty-one miles wide where the swimmers set records. Pilots would call in when leaving the island and again arriving at the far shores of Connecticut. He wore an inflatable lifejacket like others in his flying club—more veterans, no doubt. He had trained for war, not peace. The memory of battle had seeped in and set the practice. We flew the only combat-ready Beechcraft Musketeer in the sky.

That's not the way he saw it. He was just flying with the taut attention bred into him by the war. He loved to fly. Near the last of his flying days, he flew from Long Island to Florida with my mother in the Musketeer. Quite a trip for a small, single-engine airplane. How he got her to agree to that trip, we don't know. It's a marvel to us. She usually didn't fly with him. "In the back of my mind I knew I had to fly to Florida," he said. His parents, his sister, and brother-in-law were down there for the winter. "They couldn't believe I flew down there."

Somewhere over Georgia, they hit turbulence. He had been flying at 3,500 feet, a typical altitude. He checked the weather reports. "Next smooth air was at 9,000 feet. I took the little airplane up to 9,600 feet and sure enough it was as smooth as silk. And it wasn't even cold up there, which surprised the hell out of me." He was recalling his nineteen-year-old self, bundled up, gloved hands on a machine gun at the open window at twenty thousand feet.

Approaching Savannah, he radioed the tower and cut the engine, expecting the plane to drop like a stone. It didn't. "I had to auger it down, unscrew it, a little bit at a time." He slowly circled down. A golden moment. "That flight going to 9,600 feet was really something to remember. It was smooth," he said. In all the descriptions of the B-24, in flight and battle, no one ever said it was smooth.

He was planning next to fly to Quebec. He wanted to revisit the Chateau Frontenac, a trip they had taken early in their marriage. "So, I decided to bone up on my navigation and my flying skills. I took the airplane one day and got up around three hundred feet and the engine quit." A bad altitude for trouble. Altitude and airspeed are money in the bank, his old flying teacher John Bosko used to say. At three hundred feet he was almost insolvent.

"So I started punching knobs with one hand"—trying to restart the engine—and "with the other hand I declared an emergency," calling the tower. He restarted the engine. "I nursed the airplane up to pattern altitude and I landed it. Never found out what was bothering it."

He came home and had a shot of whiskey, another shadow of the Army Air Forces. They'd taught him that. Otherwise, he didn't drink at all.

"Was determined to take it up again, or as we used to say, get back on the horse that threw you." More Air Force operational practice. If you had a scare, you got back in the airplane. "Well, this horse didn't throw me, but it wanted to."

He booked the plane and flew around. "Uneventful," he said. But "you're never bored in a single-engine airplane. Flew out over Long Island Sound, did a few steep turns and that's the last time I flew. I never flew again. I didn't want to. I never discussed this with anybody," he said at age 94. That close call at three hundred feet had rattled him. He had overcome so much in his life, but this small incident had a big footprint. Was it an echo of flying through fire in 1944? I don't know. I knew him until I was sixty-two and he was ninety-four, and there is so much I don't know. "That was the end of my private pilot career," he said. The end of a lifetime's romance that started back as a city kid in the streets, looking up, wanting to fly. *Lindy! Lindy! Come on down!*

# A NOTE ON USAGE

THE AIR FORCE WENT THROUGH SEVERAL NAME CHANGES ON ITS WAY to becoming a separate military branch. As part of the Army, it was known as the Army Air Corps from 1926 to June 1941, when it became the Army Air Forces. In 1947, it was on its own as the Air Force. In this book, following the lead of several historians, I refer to the Army Air Forces or the Air Force, which was in common use during the war.

The Eighth Air Force, which fought in Europe, was reorganized as the war went on, and some of its parts were renamed. For example, the Eighth was known as "VIII Bomber Command" until the start of 1944, when it officially became the Eighth Air Force. Some of its units were known by shorter names; the Bombardment Groups were usually called Bomb Groups. I've used the most common names.

# ACKNOWLEDGMENTS

I AM INDEBTED TO AVIATION HISTORIAN JAY SPENSER FOR HIS CAREFUL review of my manuscript. Jay has seldom been far from airplanes. He was an assistant curator at the Smithsonian's National Air and Space Museum, and the curator of the Museum of Flight in Seattle. Jay is the author of *The Airplane: How Ideas Gave Us Wings*, and other books.

For their research help, I thank Carl E. Vail III; Chris Brassfield, 466th BG historian; James Edward Clarey, curator of the 453rd Bombardment Group Museum, Old Buckenham, England; Randy Asherbranner, military records researcher; Air Force Historical Research Agency; and Scott Mansfield.

My thanks to Henry Walters for his insightful reading of the manuscript.

I wouldn't get very far without Hancock Town Library Director Amy Markus and her determination to locate rare books and convince sometimes reluctant institutions to send them her way.

As always, my deepest thanks to my wife and editor, the octopus whisperer, turtle wrangler, and caretaker of good creatures, Sy Montgomery.

# BIBLIOGRAPHY

## PRIMARY SOURCES

*Air Force: The Official Service Journal of the U.S. Army Air Forces.* October 1943, January 1945.

Air Force Historical Research Agency. Mission planning, reports and analysis, 1943–1945, filed under: 0008 Air Force; Division/0002/Bombardment; Group/0453/Bombardment(Heavy); Squadron/0733/Bombardment (Heavy).

Army Air Force, 2nd Bombardment Division. *Target Victory.* Various issues, Fall 1944.

Army Air Force Historical Office. *The War Against the Luftwaffe: AAF Counter-Air Operations April 1943–June 1944.* U.S. Air Force Historical Study 110. August 1945.

Army Air Forces. *Get That Fighter.* November 1, 1943.

———. *Information File: Flexible Gunnery.* Air Forces Manual No. 20. Training Aids Division, 1944.

———. *Pilot Training Manual for the Liberator B-24.* AAF Manual No. 50-12. Revised May 1, 1945.

Assistant Chief of Air Staff, Intelligence, Historical Division. "Flexible Gunnery Training in the AAF." *Army Air Forces Historical Studies* no. 31 (March 1945).

*Browning Machine Gun, Caliber .50, AN-M2 Aircraft Basic.* War Department Technical Manual TM9-225. January 1947.

*Eighth Air Force Tactical Development.* August 1924–May 1945. July 1945.

Hastings. Donald W., et al. *Psychiatric Experiences of the Eighth Air Force. First Year of Combat (July 4, 1942–July 4, 1943).* Josiah Macy Jr. Foundation, 1943.

Hobbs, Nicholas, ed. *Psychological Research on Flexible Gunnery Training.* Report No. 11. Army Air Force Aviation Psychology Program Research Reports, 1947.

Mansfield, Pincus. Mission diary. August 4, 1944–September 10, 1944.

———. Pilot logbook. April 22, 1967–August 5, 1976.

———. Taped recollections, 2011–2019.

Mansfield, Scott. "The Meierowicz Family. A Compilation for Yizkor Remembrance." 2023.

M. P. Enlisted Record and Report of Separation. Honorable Discharge. November 20, 1945.

M. P. Hospital Admission Cards, Office of the Surgeon General, Dept. of the Army, October 1944–March 1945.

Office of Statistical Control. *Army Air Forces Statistical Digest: World War II.* December 1945.

*A Short Guide to Great Britain.* War and Navy Departments, 1943.

"Statistical Summary of Eighth Air Force Operations." *European Theater,* August 17, 1942–May 8, 1945. June 1945.

*Target: Germany. The U.S. Army's Air Forces' VIII Bomber Command's First Year over Europe.* British Edition. His Majesty's Stationery Office, 1944.

*Tyndall Field, Flexible Gunnery Class 44-8.* Army Air Forces Gunnery School. Tyndall Field Florida.

U.S. Army Air Forces. "Report of Aircraft Accident." *Mary Harriet.* Accident No. 45-09-25-522.

Vail, Carl E., Jr. Pilot logbook. June 3, 1943–December 24, 1944.

## Secondary Sources

### B-24

Birdsall, Steve. *Log of the Liberators.* Doubleday & Co., 1973.

Carigan, William. "The B-24 Liberator—A Man's Airplane." *Aerospace Historian* 35, no. 1 (Spring/March 1988).

Dorr, Robert F. *B-24 Liberator Units of the Eighth Air Force.* Osprey Publishing, 1999.

Johnsen, Frederick A. *B-24 Liberator: Rugged but Right.* McGraw-Hill, 1999.

### Eighth Air Force

Ambrose, Stephen E. *The Wild Blue: The Men and Boys Who Flew the B-24s over Germany.* Simon & Schuster, 2001.

Astor, Gerald. *The Mighty Eighth: The Air War in Europe as Told by the Men Who Fought It.* Donald I. Fine Books, 1997.

B-24 Pilot Bob Ruiz. Western Museum of Flight. https://youtu.be/9MKSJH0KNvg.

Best, Gary A. *Belle of the Brawl: Letters Home from a B-17 Bombardier.* Inkwater Press, 2010.

Caidin, Martin. *Black Thursday: The Story of the Schweinfurt Raid.* Dutton, 1960. Reprint, 2018.

Caldwell, Donald, and Richard Muller. *The Luftwaffe over Germany.* Frontline Books, 2014.

Carson, Eugene T. *Wing Ding: Memories of a Tailgunner.* Eugene T. Carson, 2000.

Freeman, Gregory A. *The Last Mission of the Wham Bam Boys.* Palgrave Macmillan, 2011.

Freeman, Roger A. "Airfields of the Eighth: Then and Now." *After the Battle Magazine,* 1978.

———. *The Mighty Eighth.* Motorbooks International, 1991.

———. *The Mighty Eighth War Diary.* Motorbooks International, 1990.

———. *The Mighty Eighth War Manual.* Cassell & Co., 2001.

Hutton, Bud (Oram C.), and Andy Rooney. *Air Gunner.* Farrar & Rhinehart, Inc.,1944.

Kaplan, Philip, and Rex Alan Smith. *One Last Look: A Sentimental Journey to the Eighth Air Force Heavy Bomber Bases of World War II in England.* Abbeville Press, 1983.

# BIBLIOGRAPHY

Miller, Donald L. *Masters of the Air: America's Bomber Boys Who Fought the Air War Against Nazi Germany.* Simon & Schuster, 2006.

Smith, Ben, Jr. *Chick's Crew: A Tale of the Eighth Air Force.* Ben Smith, Jr., 1978.

Snyder, Steve. *Shot Down: The True Story of Pilot Howard Snyder and the Crew of the B-17.* Susan Ruth. Sea Breeze Publishing, 2015.

Stewart, John L. *The Forbidden Diary: A B-24 Navigator Remembers.* McGraw-Hill, 1998.

Wolf, Kenneth. *Tail Gunner: WWII Documentary.* n.d. https://youtu.be/m9hSn1JXOdE.

## 453rd BG

The 453rd Bombardment Group Museum. http://www.453museum.com.

Alve, Eino V. *Remembrances of the Shack Rabbit.* Eino V. Alve, 1985.

Benarcik, Michael D. *In Search of Peace: A Review of the Events and Emotional Experiences Endured by the Eighth Air Force Bombardment Groups in World War II.* The Michael D. Benarcik Foundation, 1989.

Lindsley, George A., et al. *Always Out Front; The Bradley Story.* 1999. https://www.ibiblio.org/hyperwar/AAF/Bradley/Bradley-4.html.

Low, Andy. *The Liberator Men of "Old Buc": The Story of the 453rd Bombardment Group (Heavy) in World War II, 29 June 1943–15 September 1945.* Andy Low, 1979.

"Old Buckshots." Photos of Old Buckenham. https://www.flickr.com/photos/oldbuckshots/albums/72157636999226295/page3.

Potts, Ramsay. "The Reminiscences of Brigadier General Ramsay Potts." Oral History Research Office, Columbia University, 1960.

Sowter, Keith. *Aircraft of the 453rd.* Keith Sowter, 2013.

Wright, Stuart J. *An Emotional Gauntlet: From Life in Peacetime America to War in European Skies.* University of Wisconsin Press, 2008.

## Training and Wartime Films

*Combat America.* United States Army Air Forces, 1945. 1 hr. 2 min. https://youtu.be/gvbx3PhPmBU.

Enright, Ray, director. *The Rear Gunner.* Warner Bros. Pictures, 1943. 25 min. https://youtu.be/oKdLbEQ6Dv8.

*Flak.* First Motion Picture Unit, Army Air Forces, 1944. 17 min. https://youtu.be/yRd_AW1aZ8M.

*Flexible Aerial Gunnery: Making a Gunner.* War Department Training Film, 1943. 12 min. https://youtu.be/30dKkk4yaGI.

Houston, John, director. *Winning Your Wings.* Warner Bros. Pictures, 1942. 18 min. https://youtu.be/SrVVFWIHznM.

Hubley, John, director. *Position Firing.* United States Army Air Forces, 1944. 14 min. https://youtu.be/UXNBHWJXZuo.

Keighly, William, director. *Target for Today.* First Motion Picture Unit, Army Air Forces, 1944. 90 min. https://youtu.be/4A0zhSP2-tc.

Watt, Henry, director. *Target for Tonight.* Crown Film Unit, 1941. 47 min. https://www.youtube.com/watch?v=ehnjkQgFB0U.

## *Other Books and Periodicals*

"Airmen Convalesce: Bucolic Life in New Air Force Hospital Helps Speed Recovery." *Life*, July 17, 1944.

Albrecht, Brian. "World War II B-24 Gunner Got Ticket Home after Surviving Thirty Missions." *The Cleveland Plain Dealer*, March 3, 2019.

Armbruster, Ann. *The Life and Times of Miami Beach*. Alfred A. Knopf, 1995.

Baime, A. J. *The Arsenal of Democracy: FDR, Detroit, and an Epic Quest to Arm an America at War*. Houghton Mifflin Harcourt, 2014.

Barclay, Dorothy. "Air Causalities Cured at Pawling." *New York Times*, May 21, 1944.

Biddle, Tami Davis. *Rhetoric and Reality in Air Warfare: The Evolution of British and American Ideas about Strategic Bombing, 1914–1945*. Princeton University Press, 2002.

Blume, G. "Butt Report—18 August 1941." Gblume.com.

Bond, Douglas D. *The Love and Fear of Flying*. International Universities Press, 1952.

Bowyer, Michael J. F., *Action Stations, Vol. 1: Military Airfields of East Anglia, 1939–1945*. Patrick Stephens, 1979.

Brown, R. Douglas. *East Anglia 1939*. Terence Dalton Limited, 1980.

Browning, Christopher R., et al. *The United States Holocaust Memorial Museum Encyclopedia of Camps and Ghettos, 1933–1945. Volume II: Ghettos in German-Occupied Eastern Europe*. Indiana University Press, 2012.

Buderi, Robert. *The Invention that Changed the World: How a Small Group of Radar Pioneers Won the Second World War and Launched a Technical Revolution*. Simon & Schuster, 1997.

Burleigh, Michael. *Moral Combat*. HarperCollins, 2011.

Callander, Bruce D. "The Aces that History Forgot." *Air Force Magazine*, April 1991.

Carter, Kit C., and Robert Mueller, eds. *The Army Air Forces in World War II. Combat Chronology 1941–1945*. Center for Air Force History, 1991.

Correll, John T. "Daylight Precision Bombing." *Air Force Magazine*, October 2008.

———. "The Real Twelve O'Clock High." *Air Force Magazine*, January 2011.

Clark, Edie. *What There Was Not to Tell: A Story of Love and War*. Benjamin Mason Books, 2013.

Craven, Wesley Frank, and James Lea Cate, eds. *The Army Air Forces in World War II. Vol. 2: Europe: Torch to Point Blank, August 1942 to September 1943*. 1955: Office of Air Force History, 1983.

———. *Vol. 3: Europe: Argument to V-E Day, January 1944 to May 1945*. 1955: Office of Air Force History, 1983.

———. *Vol. 6: Men and Planes*, 1955: Office of Air Force History, 1983.

———. *Vol. 7: Services around the World*. 1955: Office of Air Force History, 1983.

Cronkite, Walter. *A Reporter's Life*. Alfred A. Knopf, 1996.

Davis, Richard G. *Bombing the European Axis Powers. A Historical Digest of the Combined Bomber Offensive 1939–1945*. Air University Press, 2006.

———. *Carl A. Spaatz and the Air War in Europe*. Center for Air Force History, 1993.

Devita, Frank. "D-Day." *American Veteran*. Episode 2, PBS, September 23, 2021.

Dewey, Donald. *James Stewart: A Biography*. Turner Publishing, 1996.

Doolittle, Jimmy, and Carroll V. Glines. *I Could Never Be So Lucky Again*. Bantam Books, 1991.

# BIBLIOGRAPHY

Eliot, Marc. *Jimmy Stewart: A Biography*. Harmony Books, 2006.

Fishgall, Gary. *Pieces of Time: The Life of James Stewart*. Scribner, 1997.

Forman, Wallace R. *B-17 Nose Art Name Directory*. Phalanx Publishing Co. Ltd., 1996.

———. *B-24 Nose Art Name Directory*. Phalanx Publishing Co. Ltd., 1996.

Grayling, A. C. *Among the Dead Cities*. Walker & Co., 2006.

Grigg, Erik. "Early Medieval Dykes (400 to 850 AD)." PhD thesis, School of Arts, Languages, and Cultures, 2015.

Grinker, Roy R., and John P. Spiegel. *Men Under Stress*. The Blakiston Company, 1945.

Grossman, David. *On Killing: The Psychological Cost of Learning to Kill in War and Society*. Little, Brown 1995.

Hillary, Richard. *The Last Enemy*. Macmillan & Co., 1942.

Hynes, Samuel, et al., ed. *Reporting World War II, Part Two: American Journalism 1944–46*. Library of America, 1995.

Jarrell, Mary, ed. *Randall Jarrell's Letters: An Autobiographical and Literary Selection*. Houghton Mifflin, 1985.

Jarrell, Randall. *Kipling, Auden & Co.: Essays and Reviews 1935–1964*. Farrar, Straus and Giroux, 1981.

Lay, Beirne, Jr. "Jimmy Stewart's Finest Performance." *Saturday Evening Post*, December 8 and 15, 1945.

Levine, Alan J. *The Strategic Bombing of Germany, 1940–1945*. Praeger Publishers, 1992.

Link, Mae Mills, and Hubert A. Coleman. *Medical Support of the Army Air Forces in World War II*. Office of the Surgeon General, USAF, 1955.

Matthews, Anne, et al., ed. *Reporting World War II, Part I: American Journalism, 1938–1944*. Library of America, 1995.

Maudlin, Bill. *Up Front*. 1945: W.W. Norton & Co., 1995.

Maurer, Maurer, ed. *Air Force Combat Units of World War II*. Office of Air Force History, 1983.

———. *Combat Squadrons of the Air Force: World War II*. Albert F. Simpson Historical Research Center, and Office of Air Force History, 1982.

Murray, Williamson, and Allan R. Millet. *A War to be Won: Fighting the Second World War*. Harvard University Press, 2000.

Murrow, Edward R. "Orchestrated Hell." CBS radio broadcast of Berlin Night Bombing Raid, December 3, 1943. Transcribed by Michael E. Eidenmuller. American rehetoric.com.

The National World War II Museum. "St. Louis, July 12, 1973: A Disaster with Long-Lasting Repercussions." https://www.nationalww2museum.org/war/articles/st-louis-national-records-fire-july-12-1973.

Neufeld, Michael J. *The Rocket and the Reich*. Harvard University Press, 1995.

Nijboer, Donald. *Gunner: An Illustrated History of WWII Aircraft Turrets and Gun Positions*. The Boston Mills Press, 2001.

O'Neill, Marta G., and William Seibert. "Burnt in Memory: Looking Back, Looking Forward at the 1973 St. Louis Fire." *Prologue*, Spring 2013.

Overy, Richard. *Why the Allies Won*. W. W. Norton & Co., 1995.

Pritchard, William H. *Randall Jarrell: A Literary Life*. Farrar, Straus and Giroux, 1992.

Pyle, Ernie. *Brave Men*. 1944. University of Nebraska Press, 2001.

Rochlin, Fred. *Old Man in a Baseball Cap: A Memoir of World War II*. Thorndike Press, 1999.

Rhodes, Richard. *The Making of the Atomic Bomb*. Simon and Schuster, 1986.

Rooney, Andy. *My War*. Random House, 1995.

Ross, Stewart Halsey. *Strategic Bombing by the United States in World War II: The Myths and the Facts*. McFarland & Company, 2002.

Salter, James. *Burning the Days*. Random House, 1997.

Schaffer, Ronald. *Wings of Judgment: American Bombing in World War II*. Oxford University Press, 1985.

Scott, Denton. "School for Gunners." *Yank: The Army Weekly*, February 3, 1943.

Sellers, Michael, director. *Return to Hardwick: Home of the 93rd Bomb Group*, 2019. 1 hr. 13 min.

Sherry, Michael S. *The Rise of American Air Power: The Creation of Armageddon*. Yale University Press, 1987.

Smith, Starr. *Jimmy Stewart: Bomber Pilot*. Zenith Press, 2005.

Sperber, A. M. *Murrow: His Life and Times*. Bantam Books, 1986.

Stacey, C. P. "The Bombing of Germany, 1939–1945." *International Journal* (Summer 1962).

Steinbeck, John. *Bombs Away: The Story of a Bomber Team*. The Viking Press, 1942.

———. *Once There Was a War*. The Viking Press, 1958.

Stender, Walter W., and Evans Walker. "The National Personnel Records Center Fire: A Study in Disaster." *The American Archivist*, October 1974.

Swift, Daniel. *Bomber County: The Poetry of a Lost Pilot's War*. Farrar, Straus and Giroux, 2010.

Underwood, Jeffrey S. "Gunnery Training at Tyndall Field, Florida, 1941–1945." *Air Power History*, Winter 1995.

*The Vassar Chronicle*. "Hospital at Pawling is G.I. Paradise; Men Brought Back to Health and Duty." June 24, 1944.

*Vassar Miscellany News*. "Pawling Hospital Returns Soldiers to Service through Rehabilitation." March 7, 1945.

Wells, Mark Kendall. "Aviators and Air Combat: A Study of the U.S. Eighth Air Force and R.A.F. Bomber Command." PhD thesis, University of London, 1992.

———. *Courage and Air Warfare: The Allied Aircrew Experience in the Second World War*. Frank Cass & Co, Ltd., 1995.

Werrell, Kenneth P. "The Strategic Bombing of Germany in World War II: Costs and Accomplishments." *The Journal of American History* (December 1986).

Wilson, Charles (Lord Moran). *The Anatomy of Courage*. Houghton Mifflin, 1967.

Wohl, Robert. *A Passion for Wings: Aviation and the Western Imagination, 1908–1918*. Yale University Press, 1994.

———. *The Spectacle of Flight: Aviation and the Western Imagination, 1920–1950*. Yale University Press, 2005.

Wright, David G., ed. *Observations on Combat Flying*. Josiah Macy Jr. Foundation, 1945.

# ABOUT THE AUTHOR

**Howard Mansfield** has written a dozen books, including *In the Memory House, The Same Ax, Twice, The Bones of the Earth, Turn & Jump, Dwelling in Possibility*, and the children's book *Hogwood Steps Out*.

Through his writing, Mansfield sifts through the commonplace and the forgotten to discover stories that tell us about ourselves and our place in the world. The late critic Guy Davenport said: "Howard Mansfield has never written an uninteresting or dull sentence. All of his books are emotionally and intellectually nourishing. He is something like a cultural psychologist along with being a first-class cultural historian. He is humane, witty, bright-minded, and rigorously intelligent."

His essays and articles on history and architecture have appeared in such newspapers as the *New York Times, Washington Post, Christian Science Monitor, Boston Globe, Los Angeles Times*, the *Philadelphia Inquirer*, and the *Chicago Tribune*, as well as in magazines, including *American Heritage, Metropolis, International Design, Yankee, Historic Preservation, Threepenny Review, Orion, DoubleTake*, and *Air & Space*.

Mansfield's work has been honored with a Gold Medal for Commentary for City and Regional Magazines, a Silver Medal from the Independent Publisher Book Awards, and as a Feature Story Finalist in the National City and Regional Magazine Awards. He received an honorary doctor of humane letters from Franklin Pierce University.

He lives in Hancock, New Hampshire, with his wife, the writer Sy Montgomery.